PAT
TRAVEL GUIDE
2024-2025

A land that defies expectations and ignites
the spirit of adventure

ETHEL COULTER

Copyright © 2024 by Ethel Coulter

All rights reserved. No part of this publication may be reproduced, distributed, or transmitted in any form or by any means, including photocopying, recording, or other electronic or mechanical methods, without the prior written permission of the publisher.

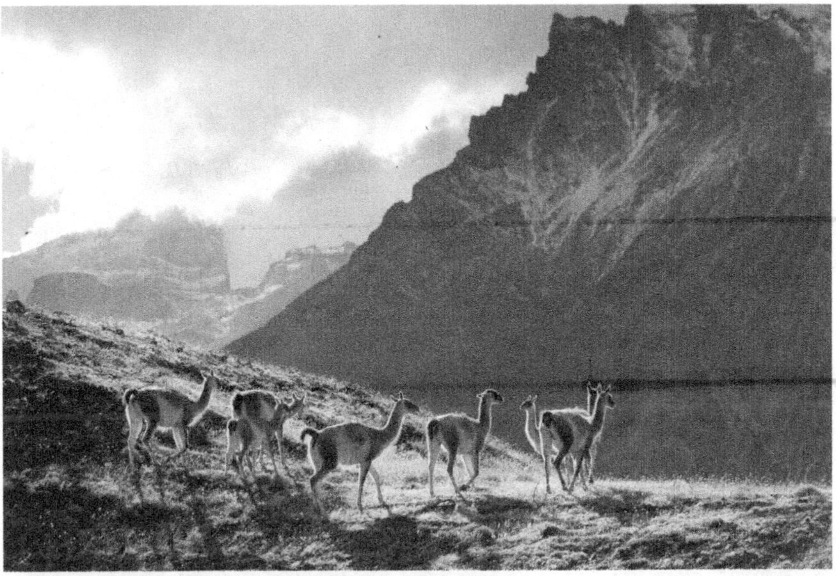

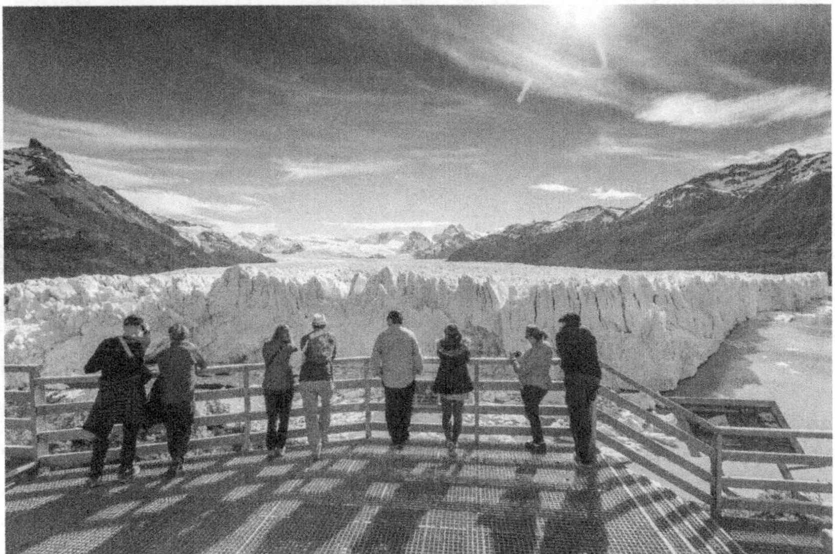

LAGO SAN MARTIN
EXCURSIONES
TRANSFERS
Prana
Bar
Natural
Casa de

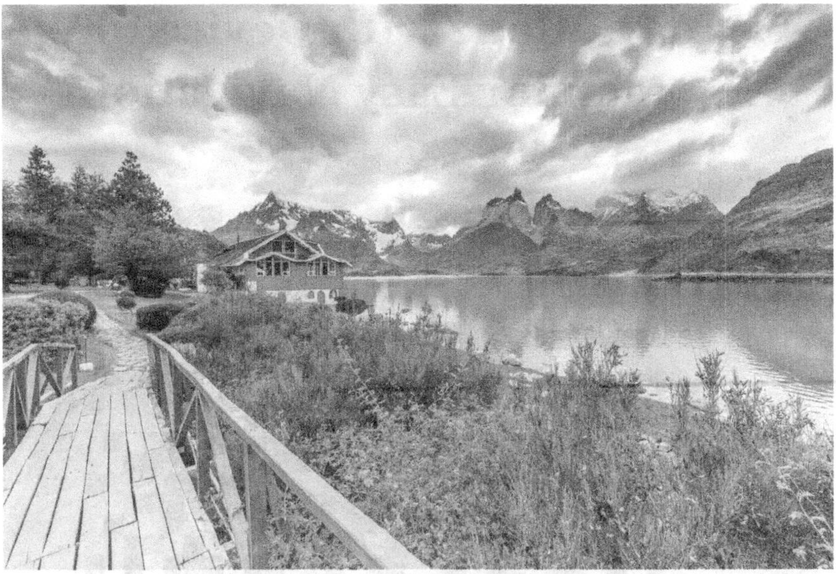

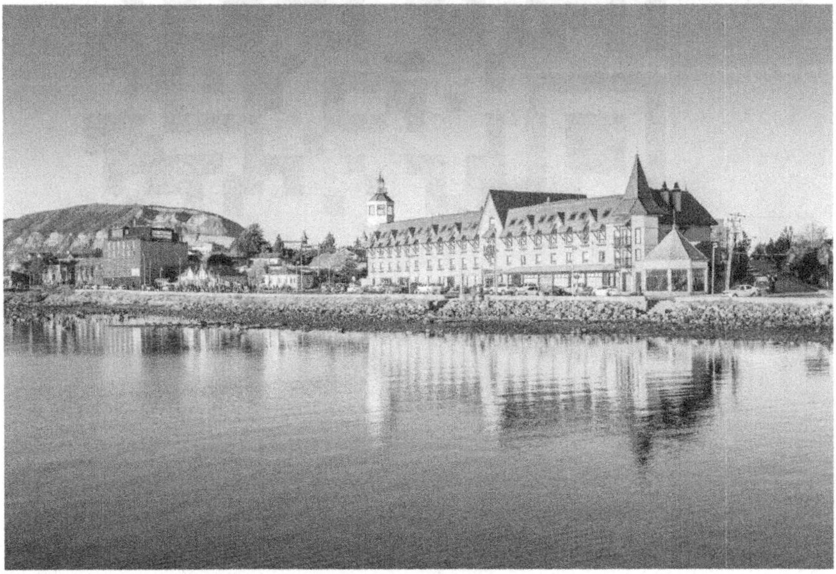

Scan QR Code with Device to View Map for Easy Navigation

CONTENTS

INTRODUCTION.. 9
    About Patagonia.. 13
    Reasons to Love Patagonia..................................... 16
    History and Culture Overview................................. 18

CHAPTER 1: PLANNING YOUR TRIP TO PATAGONIA 20
    When to visit Patagonia... 22
    How to Get to Patagonia.. 25
    Getting Around Patagonia...................................... 28
    Where to Stay: Neighborhoods in Patagonia............. 31
    What to Pack.. 34
    Entry and Visa Requirements................................. 37
    Currency and Language... 40
    Suggested Budget.. 43
    Money-Saving Tips.. 46
    Best Places to Book Your Trip................................. 50

CHAPTER 2: MUST-SEE ATTRACTIONS AND LANDMARKS.. 53
    Perito Moreno Glacier.. 54
    Torres del Paine.. 56
    Fitz Roy Mountain... 58
    Tierra del Fuego National Park............................... 61
    Península Valdés... 64
    Marble Caves.. 67
    Cueva de las Manos... 70
    Parque Nacional Nahuel Huapi.............................. 73
    Queulat Hanging Glacier....................................... 76
    Magdalena Island.. 79

CHAPTER 3: ACCOMMODATION OPTIONS......................82
Best Luxury Hotels and Resorts..83
Budget-Friendly Accommodations..85
Unique Stays and Local Favorites...88
Practical Tips for Booking Accommodations........................ 91
CHAPTER 4: DINING AND CUISINE.....................................94
Best Restaurants and Eateries..95
Local Flavors and Must-Try Dishes.. 98
Dining with a View... 101
Dining Etiquette and Local Foodie Tips...............................104

CHAPTER 5: THINGS TO DO AND OUTDOOR ACTIVITIES... 107
Hiking Trails in the Patagonia...108
Kayaking and Canoeing Adventures..................................... 110
Hot Air Balloon Rides...112
Wildlife Spotting Excursions..114
Gardens and Parks to Explore..116
Outdoor Adventure Tips...118

CHAPTER 6: ART, CULTURE AND ENTERTAINMENT.... 120
Local Arts and Crafts... 121
Museums and Galleries...123
Festivals and Events..125
Nightlife and Entertainment...128
Local Markets, Shopping, and Souvenirs............................ 130

CHAPTER 7: 7-DAY ITINERARY IN PATAGONIA...... 132
Day 1: Touchdown in Patagonia's Gateway - El Calafate..... 132
Day 2: Marveling at the Mighty Perito Moreno Glacier....... 133
Day 3: Trekking Paradise - El Chaltén..................................134
Day 4: Conquering Laguna de los Tres................................ 135
Day 5: Journey to the End of the World - Ushuaia...............135

Day 6: Exploring the Beagle Channel.................................. 136
Day 7: Farewell to Patagonia..137
CHAPTER 8: PRACTICAL INFORMATION AND TIPS 139
Etiquette and Customs in Patagonia: Dancing with the Wind.. 139
Language and Communication.. 142
Simple Language Phrases... 145
Health and Safety Tips.. 148
Emergency Contacts.. 152
Communication and Internet Access.................................. 156
Useful Apps, Websites, and Maps.. 160
CONCLUSION... 163

INTRODUCTION

Welcome, intrepid traveler, to the awe-inspiring realm of Patagonia! As you delve into this guide, let your imagination soar across a landscape where nature's raw power and beauty reign unchallenged. Picture yourself standing amidst endless pampas, where the relentless wind whispers tales of ancient glaciers and towering peaks.

This is Patagonia – a land that defies expectations and ignites the spirit of adventure. Here, colossal glaciers carve their way through pristine valleys, their icy blue faces reflecting the wild, untamed essence of the region. Jagged mountain ranges pierce the sky, their snow-capped summits beckoning to those who dare to dream big and climb high.

As you journey through this remote corner of South America, prepare to be humbled by the sheer magnitude of your surroundings. Vast grasslands stretch to the horizon, home to elusive pumas and graceful guanacos. Crystal-clear lakes mirror the ever-changing Patagonian sky, while hidden fjords reveal a world of unspoiled beauty.

My Patagonian adventure began in El Calafate, a charming town nestled on the edge of the Southern Patagonian Ice Field. The moment I stepped off the plane, I could feel the crisp, clean air filling my lungs. It was as if the worries of the world I'd left behind simply melted away. That first evening, I found myself at a cozy local restaurant, savoring a plate of lamb so tender it practically fell off the bone. As I sipped my Malbec, I chatted with fellow travelers, all of us buzzing with excitement for what lay ahead.

The next morning, I set out for the crown jewel of the region: Perito Moreno Glacier. Nothing could have prepared me for the sheer magnitude of this icy giant. As I stood on the viewing platform, the glacier seemed to stretch endlessly before me, its jagged surface a mesmerizing maze of blue and white. Suddenly, a thunderous crack split the air. I watched in awe as a massive chunk of ice calved from the glacier's face, crashing into the milky turquoise waters below. It was nature at its most raw and powerful, a moment that left me feeling humbled and alive.

Eager for a closer look, I joined a group for an ice trek on the glacier itself. Strapping on crampons and gripping an ice axe, I felt like a true explorer. Our guide led us across the glacier's surface, pointing out deep crevasses and ice formations that sparkled like diamonds in the sunlight. We paused for a break, and our guide chipped off some glacial ice for our water bottles. I've never tasted water so pure and refreshing – it was like drinking from the very veins of the earth.

From El Calafate, I journeyed north to the hiker's paradise of El Chaltén. This tiny mountain town sits in the shadow of the iconic Mount Fitz Roy, its jagged spires a siren call to adventurers from around the world. I spent my days here hiking through pristine forests and alongside crystal-clear streams, each turn in the trail revealing a new, breathtaking vista. One morning, I rose before dawn to catch the sunrise at Laguna de los Tres. The grueling final ascent was forgotten the moment the first rays of sunlight hit Fitz Roy's granite face, setting it ablaze in a brilliant orange glow. Sitting there, surrounded by fellow hikers all rendered speechless by the beauty before us, I felt a profound connection to both the landscape and my fellow travelers.

My Patagonian odyssey then took me across the border into Chile and the renowned Torres del Paine National Park. Here, I embarked on the famous W Trek, a multi-day hike that winds through some of the most stunning landscapes I've ever laid eyes on. Each day brought new wonders – from the towering granite spires of Las Torres to the otherworldly blue of Glacier Grey. I'll never forget the night I spent camping beside Lake Pehoé. As darkness fell, the Cuernos del Paine were silhouetted against a sky ablaze with more stars than I thought possible. The Milky Way stretched overhead like a river of light, and in that moment, I felt both incredibly small and part of something immeasurably vast.

The final leg of my journey took me to the very end of the continent – Ushuaia, the world's southernmost city. There's a palpable sense of adventure in this frontier town, a feeling that you're standing at the edge of the known world. I boarded a catamaran for a cruise along the Beagle Channel, where I spotted playful sea lions, colonies of cormorants, and even a pod of dolphins dancing in our wake. As we sailed past the Les Eclaireurs Lighthouse, its red and white stripes stark against the rocky shore, I couldn't help but think of the countless explorers who had passed this way before, venturing into the unknown.

My time in Patagonia was drawing to a close, but I knew a part of me would remain forever in this wild, beautiful land. From the windswept steppes to the towering peaks, from the immense glaciers to the cozy refugios where travelers gather to share stories, Patagonia had worked its way into my soul. As I boarded my flight home, my heart was full of memories I knew would last a lifetime.

Now it's your turn to experience the magic of Patagonia. Whether you're yearning for epic hikes, longing to witness nature at its most grand, or simply seeking to disconnect from the noise of everyday life, this remarkable corner of the world awaits. Pack your sense of wonder, open your heart to adventure, and prepare to fall in love with Patagonia. The journey of a lifetime begins here.

About Patagonia

Hey there! Prepare to be blown away by the breathtaking beauty of Patagonia, a place where nature shows off and adventure is always around the corner. This huge area covers the southern parts of Argentina and Chile, and it's like a patchwork of different landscapes that will make your jaw drop.

Patagonia is a geographical marvel, covering over 400,000 square miles that's roughly the size of Texas and California combined. It's a place of extremes, where the Andes Mountains plunge dramatically into the sea, creating a jagged coastline of fjords and islands. The region is home to the Southern Patagonian Ice Field, the world's third-largest freshwater reserve after Antarctica and Greenland. This massive expanse of ice feeds some of the most impressive glaciers you'll ever lay eyes on, including the advancing Perito Moreno Glacier, a rare spectacle in our warming world.

But Patagonia isn't all ice and mountains. The eastern side gives way to vast steppes, locally known as 'pampas', where hardy grasses and shrubs paint the landscape in muted hues of gold and green. These windswept plains are home to an array of unique wildlife. Keep your eyes peeled for guanacos, the wild ancestors of llamas, gracefully bounding across the grasslands. If you're lucky, you might spot a puma slinking through the underbrush or an Andean condor soaring overhead on its impressive 10-foot wingspan.

The region's name, 'Patagonia', has a fascinating origin. It's believed to come from the word 'patagón', used by explorer Ferdinand Magellan to describe the indigenous people he encountered. Legend has it that

Magellan thought these people were giants, though they were likely just taller than the average European of the time. This myth of Patagonian giants persisted in European imagination for centuries, adding to the region's mystique.

Patagonia's human history is as rich and varied as its landscapes. The indigenous Tehuelche people called this land home for thousands of years before European arrival. In the late 19th century, Patagonia became a refuge for outlaws and adventurers, including Butch Cassidy and the Sundance Kid, who spent time hiding out here. The region also attracted a surprising influx of Welsh settlers in the 1800s, establishing communities that maintain their cultural heritage to this day. You can still find Welsh tea houses in towns like Gaiman, where you might hear Welsh being spoken alongside Spanish.

The region's unique geography creates some truly remarkable weather patterns. The Andes act as a barrier to Pacific weather systems, resulting in dramatically different climates on either side of the mountain range. The western side receives abundant rainfall, supporting lush temperate rainforests, while the eastern side lies in a rain shadow, creating the arid Patagonian Desert. This stark contrast occurs over just a few miles, making Patagonia a paradise for climate scientists and weather enthusiasts.

Patagonia's waters are just as impressive as its lands. The confluence of the Pacific and Atlantic oceans creates rich marine ecosystems. The Valdés Peninsula is a crucial breeding ground for southern right whales, elephant seals, and sea lions. Off the southern tip of the continent, the treacherous waters of Cape Horn have challenged sailors for centuries, earning it the nickname "the sailor's graveyard."

For the scientifically inclined, Patagonia is a treasure trove of paleontological wonders. The region has yielded some of the most important dinosaur fossils ever discovered, including the remains of Argentinosaurus, potentially the largest land animal to have ever lived. The dry conditions of the Patagonian Desert have preserved fossils remarkably well, providing invaluable insights into prehistoric life.

In recent years, Patagonia has become a beacon of conservation efforts. The region is home to numerous national parks and protected areas, including the vast Patagonia National Park, a result of the largest private land donation in history. These conservation initiatives aim to preserve Patagonia's unique ecosystems and reintroduce species that had previously disappeared from the region.

Patagonia isn't just a place; it's a state of mind. It's where the Mapuche people believed the world's energy was concentrated. It's where Charles Darwin developed ideas that would revolutionize our understanding of life on Earth. It's where adventurers test their mettle against some of the most challenging terrains on the planet. And now, it's where you can write your own chapter in the grand story of this extraordinary land.

As you embark on your Patagonian journey, prepare to be transformed. Whether you're standing in awe before towering peaks, sharing mate with gauchos on the pampas, or simply breathing in the crisp, clean air, Patagonia will awaken something profound within you. This is a place that reminds us of our place in the natural world and invites us to connect with something greater than ourselves. Welcome to Patagonia - your adventure awaits.

Reasons to Love Patagonia

Patagonia is a land that captivates the heart and ignites the imagination. From its towering peaks to its sweeping plains, this remarkable region at the southern tip of South America offers a tapestry of experiences that leave an indelible mark on all who visit. Here's why you'll fall head over heels for Patagonia:

Breathtaking landscapes: Where else can you witness glaciers calving into turquoise lakes, jagged mountains piercing the sky, and endless steppes stretching to the horizon?

Wildlife encounters: Spot guanacos grazing on the plains, Andean condors soaring overhead, and penguins waddling along rocky shores.

World-class hiking: From the iconic Torres del Paine to the challenging trails around Mount Fitz Roy, Patagonia is a trekker's paradise.

Rich cultural heritage: Explore the fusion of indigenous Mapuche traditions with European influences, including surprising Welsh settlements.

Stargazing extraordinaire: With minimal light pollution, the night skies in Patagonia offer a celestial show like no other.

Authentic gaucho experiences: Connect with the cowboy culture of the pampas through stays at working estancias.

Pristine waters: From glacier-fed rivers to the meeting point of two oceans, Patagonia's waters offer unparalleled beauty and adventure.

Fascinating geological history: Walk in the footsteps of dinosaurs and witness the raw power of tectonic forces that shaped this land.

Extreme sports paradise: Whether it's ice climbing on glaciers or kitesurfing in the Strait of Magellan, adrenaline junkies will find their fix.

Culinary delights: Savor locally-raised lamb, freshly-caught king crab, and surprisingly good Patagonian wines.

Sense of remoteness: Experience the thrill of being at the "end of the world" and disconnect from the hustle of modern life.

Conservation success stories: Witness firsthand the positive impact of large-scale conservation efforts in preserving this unique ecosystem.

Seasonal beauty: Each season brings its own magic, from spring's wildflower blooms to autumn's fiery foliage.

Warm hospitality: Despite the sometimes harsh environment, Patagonians welcome visitors with open arms and genuine warmth.

Photographic opportunities: Every vista in Patagonia seems perfectly framed for a postcard, making it a photographer's dream.

History and Culture Overview

Patagonia's history is as rugged and captivating as its landscapes. This vast region has been home to indigenous peoples for thousands of years, with evidence of human habitation dating back at least 13,000 years. The Tehuelche, Mapuche, and Selk'nam were among the native groups who thrived in this challenging environment, developing unique cultures adapted to the harsh conditions.

European exploration of Patagonia began in the 16th century, with Ferdinand Magellan's expedition in 1520. The name "Patagonia" itself comes from Magellan's description of the native people as "Patagones," possibly referring to their large size compared to Europeans of the time. For centuries, Patagonia remained a land of myth and legend in European imagination, with tales of giants and lost cities capturing the public's fascination.

The 19th century brought significant changes to Patagonia. Both Argentina and Chile began efforts to assert control over the region, leading to conflicts with indigenous populations. This period saw the arrival of European settlers, including a surprising influx of Welsh immigrants who established communities in the Chubut Valley. These Welsh settlers left an enduring cultural legacy that can still be experienced today in towns like Trelew and Gaiman.

Patagonia's rugged terrain and remote location also made it a haven for outlaws and adventurers. Perhaps the most famous were Butch Cassidy and the Sundance Kid, who spent time hiding out in the region after fleeing the United States. Their exploits have become part of Patagonian folklore, adding to the region's mystique.

The 20th century brought further changes, with the development of the wool industry transforming vast areas of Patagonia into sheep ranches. This era saw the rise of the gaucho culture, with these skilled horsemen becoming symbols of Patagonian identity. Today, you can still experience this tradition through stays at working estancias.

In recent decades, Patagonia has emerged as a global symbol of conservation and environmental stewardship. The efforts of individuals like Douglas Tompkins, founder of The North Face, have led to the creation of vast protected areas. This commitment to preservation has become an integral part of modern Patagonian culture, with locals taking pride in their role as guardians of this unique ecosystem.

Today, Patagonian culture is a vibrant blend of indigenous traditions, European influences, and a deep connection to the land. You'll find this reflected in everything from the region's cuisine, which combines local ingredients like lamb and seafood with international influences, to its music and festivals. The spirit of Patagonia is one of resilience, adventure, and respect for nature - values that continue to shape the region and captivate visitors from around the world.

CHAPTER 1: PLANNING YOUR TRIP TO PATAGONIA

Embarking on a Patagonian adventure requires a bit of planning, but the rewards are well worth the effort. The best time to visit depends on your preferences - summer (December to February) offers milder weather and longer days, perfect for hiking, while the shoulder seasons showcase stunning autumn colors or spring blooms with fewer crowds. As you prepare for your journey, consider the vast distances involved; most travelers fly into major hubs like Punta Arenas or El Calafate, then use a combination of buses, rental cars, and domestic flights to explore the region.

Choosing where to stay is part of the fun, with options ranging from cozy hostels in adventure hubs like El Chaltén to luxurious lodges near Torres del Paine. Whether you're drawn to the rugged beauty of the Andes or the wide-open spaces of the pampas, there's a perfect base for your explorations. As you pack, remember that Patagonia's weather can be unpredictable - layers are your best friend, and don't forget sturdy hiking boots and a good raincoat.

Before you set off, make sure you're up to speed on entry requirements; while many visitors don't need visas for short stays, it's always best to check the latest regulations. The primary languages you'll encounter are Spanish and, to a lesser extent, English, though a few phrases in the local tongue will go a long way. While Patagonia isn't a budget destination, there are ways to keep costs in check, from camping to cooking your own meals with local ingredients. Whether you book through a specialized travel agency or piece together your own itinerary online, the key is to remain flexible - in Patagonia, sometimes the most memorable experiences are the unplanned ones.

When to visit Patagonia

Choosing when to visit Patagonia is like picking your favorite flavor of ice cream - there's no wrong choice, just different experiences to savor. Let's dive into the seasons and help you find your perfect Patagonian moment.

Summer (December to February) is the golden child of Patagonian travel. The days stretch long, with the sun hanging in the sky until 10 PM, giving you ample time to soak in those jaw-dropping vistas. It's prime time for hiking, wildlife watching, and outdoor adventures. But here's the scoop - everyone and their grandmother knows this, so popular spots like Torres del Paine can feel a bit like rush hour in New York. If you're dreaming of that perfect photos of Fitz Roy without a sea of colorful hiking jackets in the foreground, summer might not be your best bet.

Now, let's talk about fall (March to May). Picture this: the beech forests explode in a riot of reds, oranges, and golds. It's like Mother Nature decided to throw a fireworks show just for you. The crowds thin out, prices drop, and there's a crisp freshness in the air that makes every breath feel invigorating. Wildlife gets frisky too - it's rutting season for guanacos, so you might catch some dramatic showdowns between males. Just keep in mind that some services start winding down in late April, and snow can make an early appearance in the mountains.

Winter (June to August) is Patagonia's best-kept secret. Yes, it's cold. Yes, many hiking trails are snowbound. But hear me out - this is when you'll see Patagonia in its most raw and elemental state. The Torres del Paine horns dusted with snow against a deep blue sky is a sight that'll stay with you forever. It's also prime time for skiing, both downhill and cross-country. And get this - it's whale watching season in the Atlantic. Imagine sipping hot chocolate in Puerto Madryn while watching Southern Right Whales breach just offshore. Pure magic.

As winter melts into spring (September to November), Patagonia shakes off its slumber. The landscape bursts into bloom, with hardy wildflowers carpeting the steppe in purples, yellows, and whites. Baby animals start appearing - fuzzy guanaco crias wobbling after their mothers, and if you're lucky, you might spot a puma cub. The weather can be a mixed bag, with some days feeling like winter and others offering a sneak peek of summer. But that's part of the charm - Patagonia at its most unpredictable and alive.

Here's a little secret - October might just be the goldilocks month for Patagonia. The harsh winter winds have usually died down, the spring flowers are in full swing, and the summer crowds haven't arrived yet. Plus, you might catch the tail end of the ski season and the start of the hiking season. Enjoy the best of both worlds without sacrificing practicality.

But wait, there's more! Each month brings its own special events. In January, you've got the Fiesta Nacional del Salmon in Chubut, where you can watch locals try to catch salmon with their bare hands. March brings the Fiesta Nacional del Trekking in El Chaltén, a celebration of all things hiking. And if you find yourself in Punta Arenas in December, don't miss the Festival of the Three Kings - a uniquely Patagonian Christmas celebration.

Now, a word to the wise - Patagonia's weather is as changeable as a teenager's mood. You could experience four seasons in one day, regardless of when you visit. That's not a bug, it's a feature! It's part of what makes this place so special and keeps you on your toes.

So, when should you visit Patagonia? Whenever the opportunity arises, the solution is straightforward and uncomplicated.. Each season paints this incredible landscape in a different light, offers unique experiences, and will leave you with memories to last a lifetime. Whether you're snowshoeing under the winter stars, watching spring bring the steppe to life, basking in the endless summer days, or marveling at the autumn colors, Patagonia has something magical in store for you.

Patagonia, it's not just about the destination, but also about embracing the journey and whatever Mother Nature throws your way. So pack your sense of adventure, bring clothes for all weather, and get ready for the trip of a lifetime - whenever you choose to come.

How to Get to Patagonia

Alright, adventurers, let's talk about getting to Patagonia. Think of it as the opening act to your grand Patagonian adventure - a bit of a journey, but oh so worth it!

First things first, unless you're a sea captain or a really ambitious cyclist, you're probably going to be flying into Patagonia. Now, here's where it gets interesting. Patagonia is huge - we're talking about an area roughly the size of France and Germany combined so your entry point depends on which part of this vast wilderness you're itching to explore.

If the Chilean side of Patagonia is calling your name, you'll likely be touching down in Punta Arenas. This city, perched on the Strait of Magellan, is about as far south as you can go before hitting Antarctica. Fun fact: on a clear day, you can sometimes see the mountains of Tierra del Fuego from the airport runway. Talk about a dramatic arrival!

For those drawn to the Argentine side, El Calafate is your probable gateway. This little town has gone from a sleepy outpost to a bustling tourist hub, all thanks to its proximity to the jaw-dropping Perito Moreno Glacier. The airport here is named after Argentina's beloved folk singer Comandante Armando Tola maybe learn one of his songs for your flight in?

But wait, there's more! If you're aiming for the northern reaches of Patagonia, Bariloche in Argentina or Puerto Montt in Chile might be your landing spots. Bariloche's airport has one of the trickiest approaches in South America, threading between mountain peaks. It's like a roller coaster ride before your feet even touch the ground!

Now, here's a pro tip: consider flying into one country and out of another. Maybe start your journey in Punta Arenas and end it in El Calafate, or vice versa. It's a great way to see more of Patagonia without backtracking. Just remember, you might need to pay a reciprocity fee when entering Argentina - think of it as your ticket to tango in the land of gauchos.

For the truly adventurous (and time-rich), why not make the journey part of the adventure? You could fly into Santiago or Buenos Aires and then take the scenic route south. In Chile, that means hopping on the Carretera Austral, a highway that winds through some of the most pristine wilderness on the planet. On the Argentine side, iconic Route 40 stretches all the way from the northern border with Bolivia down to Patagonia. It's like Route 66, but with more guanacos and mate tea stops.

If you're coming from Europe, here's a quirky option: fly to the Falkland Islands (or Islas Malvinas, depending on who you ask) and then catch a weekly flight to Punta Arenas. It's not the quickest route, but imagine the stories you'll have!

For those really looking to make an entrance, how about sailing in? Several cruise lines offer routes that include Patagonian ports. You could be sipping cocktails on deck one day and hiking up to a glacier the next. Just be prepared for the Drake Passage - it's known as the "sailor's graveyard" for a reason!

Once you've made it to your Patagonian starting point, the real fun begins. Domestic flights can whisk you between major hubs, but don't discount the buses. Yes, the journeys can be long, but the views are out of this world. Where else can you watch guanacos gallop alongside your window for hours on end?

Getting to Patagonia is just the beginning. This wild, wind-swept land has a way of capturing hearts and sparking wanderlust. Don't be surprised if you start planning your return trip before you've even left!

So pack your sense of adventure (and maybe some motion sickness pills for those mountain roads), and get ready for the journey of a lifetime. Whether you're flying, driving, sailing, or some combination of the three, the path to Patagonia is as thrilling as the destination itself. Buen viaje, adventurers!

Getting Around Patagonia

Let's talk about navigating the vast wilderness of Patagonia. Getting around this stunning region is an adventure in itself, filled with breathtaking views and unexpected encounters. Buckle up, because this ride is going to be as wild as the landscape!

First off, let's address the elephant in the room - Patagonia is enormous. We're talking about a region that could swallow up entire European countries. So, forget about seeing it all in one go. The key here is to pick your battles (or in this case, your destinations) and embrace the journey between them.

Buses are the unsung heroes of Patagonian travel. These long-distance coaches are like land cruises, complete with comfy reclining seats and sometimes even hot meals. The routes between major towns are well-established, and it's a great way to meet locals and fellow travelers. Just be prepared for some marathon journeys - the trip from Bariloche to El Calafate, for instance, can take up to 30 hours. But hey, where else can you watch the landscape transform from Alpine-like forests to vast steppes all from the comfort of your seat?

If you're short on time (or patience), domestic flights are your friend. The network of regional airports has expanded in recent years, making it easier to hop between highlights. But here's the catch - flights can be pricey, especially in high season, and they're subject to Patagonia's notoriously fickle weather. A pro tip: build some flexibility into your itinerary. That way, a delayed flight becomes an opportunity for an unexpected adventure rather than a wrench in your plans.

Now, for those who want to channel their inner gaucho, renting a car is a fantastic option. The freedom to stop at that picturesque viewpoint or detour to a hidden gem is priceless. Just keep in mind that distances between gas stations can be vast, so fill up whenever you can. Oh, and those poker-straight roads across the pampas? They're hypnotic. Take regular breaks to stay alert - and to soak in the endless horizons.

Here's something cool - in some parts of Patagonia, boats aren't just a fun option, they're a necessity. The Chilean fjords are a maze of islands and channels, where ferries are as common as buses. The Navimag ferry from Puerto Montt to Puerto Natales is like a mini-cruise, complete with whale sightings if you're lucky. And in Tierra del Fuego, you might find yourself on a boat crossing the Strait of Magellan, retracing the route of famous explorers.

For adventurous souls, hitchhiking is still a thing in Patagonia. It's more common on the Chilean side, especially along the Carretera Austral. Just be prepared for long waits and bring plenty of patience - and snacks!

Cycling is gaining popularity too. The wide-open roads and stunning scenery make for an epic bike tour. Just be ready for the infamous Patagonian winds - they can either be your best friend or your worst enemy, depending on which way you're headed.

Now, let's talk about some of the quirkier ways to get around. In Torres del Paine, you can hire horses to trek between camps. Imagine galloping across the pampas, feeling like a real Patagonian cowboy. Or how about a zodiac boat ride to get up close to the Perito Moreno Glacier? Nothing beats the thrill of navigating between icebergs.

One of the most unique experiences is the 'end of the world train' in Ushuaia. This narrow-gauge railway once carried prisoners to the local jail, but now it carries tourists into the stunning Tierra del Fuego National Park. It's like riding a piece of history through some of the most southerly forests on the planet.

In Patagonia, getting there is half the fun. That bumpy dirt road might lead to the most spectacular view you've ever seen. The long bus ride could result in a friendship that lasts a lifetime. And sometimes, the best experiences come when things don't go according to plan.

So embrace the journey, take the scenic route, and don't be afraid to mix it up. Combine a flight with a ferry ride, or a bus trip with a horse trek. In Patagonia, the way you travel is as much a part of the adventure as the destinations themselves. Happy trails!

Where to Stay: Neighborhoods in Patagonia

Welcome to the world of Patagonian accommodations, where your pillow might come with a view of towering peaks or endless steppes. Choosing where to rest your head in this vast wilderness is all part of the adventure, so let's explore some of the most captivating neighborhoods and lodging options across this remarkable region.

Let's kick things off in El Calafate, the gateway to Los Glaciares National Park. This once-sleepy town has blossomed into a vibrant hub for glacier enthusiasts. The main drag, Avenida del Libertador, is where you'll find a mix of cozy hostels and upscale hotels. But here's a tip: look for accommodation in the quieter residential areas near Lago Argentino. You might just wake up to find flamingos strutting past your window!

Now, if you're dreaming of those iconic Fitz Roy views, El Chaltén is your spot. This tiny mountain village is basically one big "neighborhood" of hikers and climbers. Most accommodations are simple but comfortable - after all, you're here for the trails, not the thread count. For a truly unique experience, book a stay at one of the remote estancias just outside town. Imagine swapping trail stories around a campfire under the Milky Way.

Crossing over to the Chilean side, Puerto Natales serves as the jumping-off point for Torres del Paine National Park. The Pedro Montt area is the lively heart of town, packed with gear shops and cozy cafes. But for a more local vibe, check out the colorful houses and small guesthouses in the quieter streets leading down to the fjord.

Speaking of Torres del Paine, why not stay right in the park? From rustic refugios to luxury eco-lodges, there's something for every style and budget. Imagine unzipping your tent to a view of the park's namesake towers, or sipping Pisco Sour on the deck of a lodge overlooking Lago Grey.

For a taste of Patagonian city life, Punta Arenas is your go-to. The Plaza de Armas is the historic heart of the city, surrounded by grand buildings from the wool boom era. Stay here for easy access to museums and restaurants. But for killer views of the Strait of Magellan, look for accommodations on the hill in the Cerro de la Cruz neighborhood.

Up in the northern reaches of Patagonia, Bariloche offers a completely different vibe. This alpine-style town hugs the shores of Lago Nahuel Huapi. The Centro Cívico area puts you in the heart of the action, but for a more tranquil stay, look to the lakeside neighborhoods like Playa Bonita or Llao Llao. You might find yourself in a Swiss-style chalet with a view that's pure Patagonia.

Now, let's talk about some truly off-the-beaten-path options. How about staying in a Kawésqar ruka (traditional hut) in the remote fjords of western Patagonia? Or bedding down in a lighthouse keeper's house on a tiny island in the Beagle Channel?

For the ultimate Patagonian experience, consider a stay at an estancia. These working sheep ranches offer a glimpse into the life of Patagonian gauchos. Some, like the famous Estancia Cristina, are only accessible by boat, adding an extra layer of adventure to your stay.

If you're exploring the Carretera Austral, the town of Coyhaique makes a great base. It's got a frontier feel, with a unique pentagonal plaza at its heart. Look for lodgings near here, or venture a bit out of town for farm stays that'll have you collecting your own eggs for breakfast.

Don't overlook Patagonia's island communities either. In Chiloé, you can stay in colorful palafitos - houses on stilts over the water in Castro or Ancud. Over in Tierra del Fuego, the port city of Ushuaia offers everything from backpacker hostels to five-star hotels, many with views of the Beagle Channel.

In Patagonia, your accommodation is more than just a place to sleep. It's a crucial part of your experience, a cozy haven after a day of exploration, and often a destination in itself. Whether you're camping under the stars, cozying up in a mountain lodge, or living it up gaucho-style on an estancia, where you stay will shape your Patagonian adventure. So choose wisely, but also be open to surprises - sometimes the most unassuming places offer the warmest welcomes and the most unforgettable stories.

What to Pack

Alright, fellow adventurers, let's talk about packing for Patagonia. This isn't your average vacation packing list - we're preparing for a place where you might experience four seasons in one day and where the wind can blow you off your feet (literally!). So, grab your favorite travel bag, and let's dive in!

First things first - layers are your new best friend. Patagonia's weather is as unpredictable as a soap opera plot twist. That sunny morning can turn into a chilly afternoon faster than you can say "guanaco." Start with a good base layer - merino wool is fantastic if you can swing it. It keeps you warm, wicks away sweat, and bonus: it doesn't get stinky as quickly as other fabrics. Undoubtedly, your tent-mates will express their gratitude for your thoughtful actions.

Now, let's talk about the holy grail of Patagonian wear - a good waterproof jacket. This isn't just about staying dry; it's your armor against the infamous Patagonian wind. Look for something breathable with a hood. And here's a pro tip: bright colors aren't just fashion statements here. They pop in photos against the dramatic landscapes and can help rescuers spot you if you decide to channel your inner explorer a bit too enthusiastically.

Footwear is crucial. You'll want sturdy, waterproof hiking boots that are already broken in. Your feet will be your primary mode of transport in many parts of Patagonia, so treat them well. Pack some comfy camp shoes too - your feet will crave them after a long day on the trails.

Here's something many people forget - a good hat and gloves. The sun can be intense (yes, even when it's cold), and the wind can make your ears feel like they're auditioning for a role in "Frozen." A warm beanie for chilly nights and a sun hat for bright days are must-haves. As for gloves, look for a pair that's warm but also allows you to use your camera or phone without taking them off.

Speaking of the sun - don't underestimate it. The ozone layer is thinner down here, so the sun packs a punch. A high SPF sunscreen, lip balm with SPF, and quality sunglasses are non-negotiable. Your future self will thank you when you're not sporting the "lobster look" in all your photos.

Now, let's get to some items you might not think of but will be oh-so-glad you packed. A good daypack is essential for hikes and excursions. Look for one with a rain cover built-in - it'll keep your snacks dry when those surprise showers hit.

Bring a reusable water bottle - and make it a big one. Patagonia's tap water is generally safe to drink, and you'll want to stay hydrated on those long hikes. Some trails have streams where you can refill, but pack water purification tablets just in case.

Here's a quirky one - pack a clothesline. Many accommodations in Patagonia don't have dryers, and that Patagonian wind is nature's tumble dryer. Just make sure to use strong clothespins, or you might find your underwear becoming a new flag on top of Fitz Roy.

Don't forget a good book or e-reader. Patagonian evenings can be long, especially in the summer when the sun doesn't set until late. It's the perfect time to dive into that novel about Patagonian explorers or brush up on your Spanish.

A power bank is a must. Outlets can be scarce on multi-day treks, and you don't want your camera dying just as that puma decides to make an appearance.

Now, here's something many travelers overlook - cash. While larger towns have ATMs, they can run out of money (especially on weekends), and many smaller places only accept cash. Bring a mix of dollars and local currency.

Pack some basic first aid supplies, including blister plasters. Your feet will face challenges they never knew existed, and you don't want a tiny blister to ruin your big hike.

Lastly, don't forget to pack your sense of adventure and a good dose of flexibility. Patagonia has a way of throwing curveballs, but those unexpected detours often lead to the best stories.

Entry and Visa Requirements

Let's dive into the nitty-gritty of getting yourself legally into Patagonia. Don't worry, it's not as daunting as scaling Fitz Roy, but it does require a bit of prep work. Think of it as the paperwork warm-up before your big adventure!

First things first - Patagonia isn't a country (wouldn't that be something?). It's a region shared by Chile and Argentina. This means you'll need to check the entry requirements for whichever country you're entering first. The good news? Both countries are pretty welcoming to tourists.

Let's start with Chile. For many travelers, including those from the US, Canada, and most European countries, Chile has a "visa-free" policy. This means you can waltz in without applying for a visa beforehand. You'll get a cute little tourist card upon arrival, valid for up to 90 days. Don't lose it - it's your ticket out of the country!

Argentina is similarly chill about tourists. Individuals from various countries are granted visa-free entry for a period of up to 90 days.. They used to charge a reciprocity fee for some countries (looking at you, USA), but they've waved goodbye to that policy. It's like they're rolling out the red carpet for you!

Now, here's where it gets interesting. If you're planning to hop between Chilean and Argentine Patagonia (and trust me, you should), you'll be crossing borders. Each time you enter a country, you start a new 90-day clock. It's like a time-traveling adventure, minus the DeLorean!

But wait, there's more! Some nationalities do need to apply for visas in advance. If you're from certain African, Asian, or Middle Eastern countries, you might need to jump through a few more hoops. Check with the Chilean or Argentine embassy in your home country well in advance. They're usually happy to help and might even throw in some travel tips!

Here's a quirky fact - if you're entering Chile, you might be asked about bringing in agricultural products. They're super strict about this. That apple you grabbed at the airport? It could land you in hot water. Best to munch it before you land or declare it. Chile takes its ecosystem seriously, and who can blame them? Have you seen how gorgeous Patagonia is?

For Argentina, they're more interested in how much cash you're bringing in. There's no limit, but if it's over $10,000, you need to declare it. Unless you're planning to buy a herd of guanacos, you probably don't need to worry about this one.

Now, let's talk about passports. Both countries require that your passport be valid for at least six months beyond your planned stay. It's like they're giving you a not-so-subtle hint to extend your trip. And make sure you have a few blank pages - those entry stamps are like badges of honor for travelers!

Here's something cool - if you're feeling really adventurous, you could arrive by sea. Several cruise ships visit Patagonian ports. If you're not disembarking, you might not even need to go through immigration. It's like being a Patagonia window-shopper!

For the digital nomads out there, both Chile and Argentina have been flirting with the idea of digital nomad visas. These aren't in place yet, but keep an eye out. Imagine working with a view of the Torres del Paine, right?

One last thing - travel insurance. Although obtaining a visa is not mandatory, acquiring one is strongly advised. Patagonia is wild in more ways than one, and you don't want a twisted ankle on a remote trail to turn into a financial disaster.

visa rules can change faster than Patagonian weather. Always check the official government websites or contact the embassies for the most up-to-date info before you go. And if all this paperwork talk has you stressed, just imagine the reward - you're going to freaking Patagonia! A little bureaucracy is a small price to pay for the adventure of a lifetime.

So there you have it - your ticket to legally exploring one of the most stunning regions on Earth. Now go forth, get those papers in order, and get ready for glaciers, guanacos, and grandeur. Patagonia is waiting!

Currency and Language

First up, let's talk about money. Patagonia is a tale of two currencies - the Chilean Peso and the Argentine Peso. Now, here's where it gets interesting. These two pesos are about as different as chalk and cheese. The Chilean Peso is relatively stable, while the Argentine Peso... well, let's just say it likes to keep things exciting. Exchange rates can change faster than a guanaco can sprint, so keep an eye on them.

In Chile, you'll find that credit cards are widely accepted in towns and cities. But once you venture into the wilds of Torres del Paine or along the Carretera Austral, cash is king. ATMs can be as elusive as the Patagonian puma in remote areas, so stock up in larger towns.

Argentina, on the other hand, has a whole different financial ecosystem. Due to the country's economic quirks, you might hear whispers about a "blue dollar" or "dólar blue." This is the unofficial exchange rate for US dollars, often much more favorable than the official rate. While not exactly legal, it's a common practice. Just be cautious and use reputable sources if you decide to dabble in this financial tango.

Now, let's chat about the lingo. Spanish is the main language in both Chilean and Argentine Patagonia. But hold onto your hats, because Patagonian Spanish throws some curveballs. In Chile, they speak at what seems like warp speed and have a knack for dropping consonants. "¿Cómo estai?" (How are you?) becomes something closer to "¿Cómo tai?" In their pursuit of verbal efficiency, their conversations resemble a contest to determine who can utter the most words while minimizing lip movement.

Argentine Spanish, particularly in Patagonia, has its own flair. They use "vos" instead of "tú" for "you," and their double-L sound is pronounced like "sh" instead of "y." So "llama" (the animal) sounds more like "shama." And don't get startled if someone calls you "boludo" - it's often used as a term of endearment among friends, kind of like "dude" in English.

But wait, there's more! Patagonia is home to several indigenous languages too. In the north, you might hear Mapudungun, the language of the Mapuche people. Words like "Neuquén" and "Lanín" (names of a province and a volcano) come from this ancient tongue. In the far south, there are still a handful of speakers of Yaghan, one of the southernmost languages in the world. Fun fact: the Yaghan word "mamihlapinatapai" is considered one of the most untranslatable words, roughly meaning "a look shared by two people, Both desired something, but neither wanted to be the one to initiate it, resulting in a stalemate where each yearned for the other to make the first move.

Now, let's talk about some Patagonian slang that'll make you sound like a local. In Argentine Patagonia, a strong wind is often called a "Viento Blanco" (White Wind), while in Chile, you might hear it referred to as "Escoba de Dios" (God's Broom). If something's really far away, Chileans might say it's "donde el diablo perdió el poncho" (where the devil lost his poncho).

When it comes to tipping, it's generally expected in restaurants (about 10% in Argentina and 10-15% in Chile). But here's a quirky tidbit - in some remote areas of Chilean Patagonia, locals might refuse tips, seeing it as charity. A heartfelt "gracias" can sometimes be more appreciated than a few extra pesos.

Oh, and if you're a coffee lover, be prepared for a linguistic adventure. In Chile, asking for a "café con leche" (coffee with milk) might get you a blank stare. Try asking for a "cortado" instead. In Argentina, a "cortado" is different again, and you might want to ask for a "lágrima" for a milky coffee.

don't be surprised if you hear a bit of Welsh in Patagonia! Yes, you read that right. There are Welsh-speaking communities in Chubut Province, Argentina. You might stumble upon a tea house where "bore da" (good morning) is as common as "buenos días."

Language is about communication, not perfection. Patagonians are generally patient and appreciative of any attempt to speak Spanish. And when words fail, a smile and some enthusiastic gesturing go a long way. After all, the language of awe is universal, and in Patagonia, you'll be speaking it fluently from the moment you arrive!

Suggested Budget

Let's talk about money, honey! Budgeting for Patagonia can be as wild as the landscape itself. But don't worry, we'll break it down so you can focus on breaking in those hiking boots instead of breaking the bank.

First things first, Patagonia isn't exactly a bargain basement destination. It's more champagne views on a beer budget kind of place. But with some savvy planning, you can make your pesos stretch further than a guanaco's leap.

Let's start with accommodation. In popular spots like El Calafate or Puerto Natales, a bed in a hostel dorm will set you back about $15-20 per night. If you're more into private rooms, budget around $50-80. Now, if you're feeling fancy and want to wake up to glacier views, luxury lodges can soar well over $300 a night. But hey, you can't put a price on waking up to a million-dollar view, right?

Camping is where the real savings are. Many national parks have campsites for as little as $5-10 per night. Plus, you get the added bonus of falling asleep under the Milky Way. Just remember, those Patagonian winds don't mess around, so invest in a good tent!

Now, let's chew over food costs. In towns, a hearty meal at a local restaurant might cost $10-15. But if you're craving a juicy Patagonian lamb feast, prepare to shell out $20-30. Cooking for yourself? A grocery run for simple meals might cost about $30-40 for a few days. And here's a hot tip: local markets often have the best deals on fresh produce.

Transportation costs can significantly impact your financial plan. A long-distance bus ride, say from Bariloche to El Calafate, could cost around $50-70. Flights between major Patagonian hubs might run you $100-200 one way. Renting a car? Budget about $50-80 per day, plus fuel costs. Remember, distances in Patagonia are vast, so factor in plenty for getting around.

Now for the fun stuff – activities! Many of Patagonia's natural wonders are free to explore, but national park entrance fees can add up. Torres del Paine will set you back about $35 in high season. A guided trek on Perito Moreno Glacier? Around $100. Whale watching in Peninsula Valdes? About $80. But trust me, these experiences are worth every peso.

Let's break it down into daily budgets:

Shoestring: $40-60 per day
This is for the hardy backpackers. We're talking dorm beds, cooking your own meals, camping, and buses. You'll need to pick and choose your paid activities carefully.

Mid-range: $100-150 per day
This gets you private rooms in hostels or budget hotels, eating out regularly, a mix of public transport and some car rental, and a good selection of activities.

Luxury: $250+ per day
Now we're talking fancy lodges, gourmet meals, internal flights or a rental car, and whatever activities your heart desires.

Remember, these are just ballpark figures. Your actual costs will depend on your travel style, the season (prices skyrocket in peak summer months), and how much you move around.

Here's a quirky Patagonian budget hack: learn to drink mate. This caffeine-packed herbal tea is not just a cultural experience, it's also a great way to make friends and potentially score some local tips or even a ride!

Another money-saving tip: look for "menu del día" options in local restaurants. These set menus often offer great value and a taste of local cuisine.

And here's something many travelers overlook: factor in some buffer money. Patagonia has a way of tempting you with unexpected adventures. Maybe you'll fall in love with horse riding and want an extra day at an estancia, or perhaps you'll hear about a hidden hot spring that's a bit out of the way. Having some flexibility in your budget allows you to say "yes" to these magical Patagonian moments.

In Patagonia, some of the best things are free. Watching a Magellanic woodpecker in the Patagonian forest, feeling the spray of a glacier on your face, or simply standing in awe of the Andes these are the priceless experiences that make Patagonia truly special.

So, pack your sense of adventure (and a calculator), and get ready for a trip that's rich in experiences, if not always light on the wallet. After all, in Patagonia, the best currency is wonder, and that, my friend, is always in abundant supply!

Money-Saving Tips

Alright, savvy travelers, let's talk about stretching your pesos in Patagonia! This stunning region might seem like a budget-buster, but with a few clever tricks, you can save some serious cash without skimping on the adventure. So, grab your wallet and let's dive into some money-saving magic!

First up, timing is everything. If you can swing it, visit during the shoulder seasons (October-November or March-April). Not only will you dodge the peak season crowds, but you'll also find lower prices on accommodation and tours. Plus, you get the bonus of seeing Patagonia dressed in either spring blooms or autumn colors. Win-win!

Now, let's talk about lodging. Hostels are great, but have you considered homestays? Many Patagonian families open their homes to travelers, offering a cozy bed, home-cooked meals, and priceless local insights for a fraction of hotel costs. It's like having a Patagonian grandmother, complete with mates and travel tips!

Speaking of mate, this local beverage is your ticket to budget-friendly socializing. Bring a thermos of hot water and your mate gourd to parks or plazas. You're bound to find locals happy to share their yerba mate and conversation. It's like a free cultural exchange program!

For food, local markets are your best friends. Not only are they cheaper than supermarkets, but they're also a feast for the senses. Challenge yourself to cook with unfamiliar local ingredients. Calafate berry jam, anyone? Your taste buds and financial well-being will express gratitude for your choice.

Here's a quirky tip: befriend some sheep farmers. No, really! Many estancias (ranches) offer work-stay programs where you can exchange a few hours of work for free accommodation and meals. It's a unique way to experience Patagonian life and save some serious dough.

Transportation can be a budget-buster, but here's a local secret: truck-sharing. In remote areas, it's common for locals to hitch rides with long-distance truck drivers. It's not the most glamorous way to travel, but it's cheap and offers a chance to practice your Spanish with some colorful characters.

For activities, look for free walking tours in cities like Punta Arenas or Ushuaia. They're often run by passionate locals and operate on a tip basis. It's a great way to get oriented and gather insider tips for the rest of your stay.

Now, let's talk about national parks. While entrance fees can add up, many parks offer multi-day passes that work out cheaper than paying daily. In Torres del Paine, for example, a 3-day pass is only slightly more expensive than a 1-day pass. More bang for your buck!

Here's a tip many travelers overlook: bring some U.S. dollars or Euros. In Argentina especially, you might get better exchange rates for foreign currency than using ATMs or credit cards. Just be sure to exchange money through reputable sources.

For souvenir shopping, skip the tourist traps and head to local craft markets. You'll find unique, handmade items often cheaper than mass-produced trinkets. Plus, you're supporting local artisans. That alpaca sweater isn't just cozy; it's got a story!

If you're into photography, consider renting gear instead of buying. Many shops in larger towns rent out high-quality cameras and lenses. You get to capture those epic Patagonian vistas without the long-term investment.

Here's a fun one: learn to identify edible plants. With a good guidebook (or a knowledgeable local), you can forage for calafate berries, wild strawberries, or even mushrooms. It's like a treasure hunt that ends with a free meal!

For those long bus journeys, pack your own snacks. Bus station food is often overpriced and underwhelming. A DIY sandwich and some local fruits will keep both your belly and budget happy.

If you're feeling adventurous, try hitchhiking. It's relatively common and generally safe in Patagonia, especially along popular routes like the Carretera Austral. Just be prepared for long waits and bring a good book.

embrace the art of slow travel. Rushing from place to place not only costs more but also means you miss out on the subtle magic of Patagonia. Sometimes, the best experiences come from simply sitting by a lake and watching the clouds roll over the mountains. And that, my friend, is absolutely free.

traveling on a budget in Patagonia doesn't mean missing out. It often means traveling deeper, connecting more with locals, and having the kind of authentic experiences that money can't buy. So pack your sense of adventure, your flexible attitude, and get ready to experience the wonders of Patagonia without breaking the bank. After all, the best things in Patagonia – the jaw-dropping landscapes, the star-filled skies, the warm local hospitality – are priceless.

Best Places to Book Your Trip

Ready to turn your Patagonian dreams into reality? Let's dive into the best ways to book your epic adventure to the end of the world. Buckle up, because planning a trip to Patagonia can be as exhilarating as the journey itself!

First up, let's talk about flights. While big-name sites like Expedia or Kayak are solid choices, don't overlook local South American airlines. LATAM, for instance, often has deals that don't show up on international search engines. Plus, they've got an extensive network within Patagonia. Pro tip: their "LATAM Pass" program can score you some sweet discounts if you're planning multiple flights.

For a uniquely Patagonian experience, check out Aerolíneas Argentinas' "Visit Patagonia" pass. It's like a golden ticket to hop between Patagonian cities at a fraction of the cost of booking separate flights. Just remember, flexibility is key with these passes - perfect for those who like to go where the Patagonian wind takes them!

Now, onto accommodation. While Booking.com and Airbnb are reliable standbys, consider some regional alternatives. In Chile, Chiletur.com offers a wide range of lodgings, from cozy cabañas to luxury lodges, often at better rates than international sites. For Argentina, Despegar.com is a treasure trove of local stays, including some off-the-beaten-path gems you won't find elsewhere.

Here's a quirky option: how about staying in a repurposed shipping container? Websites like Xpand.com.ar list unique accommodations across Patagonia, including container hotels with million-dollar views. It's like glamping, but with a cool, industrial twist!

For those seeking a truly immersive experience, check out WWOOF (World Wide Opportunities on Organic Farms). They connect travelers with organic farms and eco-projects across Patagonia. Imagine learning to shear sheep or make artisanal cheese while staying for free on a Patagonian estancia. It's like a cultural exchange program and a money-saving hack rolled into one!

Adventure seekers, listen up! While you can book many excursions on the ground, some popular treks and tours fill up fast. Websites like Swoop Patagonia specialize in Patagonian adventures and can hook you up with reputable local operators. They're particularly handy for bucket-list experiences like ice-hiking on Perito Moreno or sailing through the Beagle Channel.

For a more grassroots approach, Patagonia.com (yes, the outdoor gear company!) has a brilliant platform called "Patagonia Park Tours." They connect travelers with local guides and conservation projects. It's a great way to ensure your tourism dollars directly benefit local communities and environments.

Now, here's an insider tip: join Patagonia-focused Facebook groups like "Backpacking Patagonia" or "Patagonia on a Budget." These communities are goldmines of up-to-date info, and members often share deals on accommodations or tours. Plus, it's a great way to find travel buddies if you're flying solo.

If you're road-tripping through Patagonia (highly recommended!), check out Denomades.com for car rentals. They compare prices across multiple local agencies, often finding deals that international sites miss.

And bonus - they're experts in the unique challenges of Patagonian driving, like unpaved roads and sparse gas stations.

For those who prefer to leave the planning to the experts, consider local tour operators like Say Hueque in Argentina or Chile Nativo in Chile. They can craft custom itineraries that blend iconic sights with off-the-radar experiences. It's like having a Patagonian best friend plan your trip!

Here's a wild card: Couchsurfing is alive and well in Patagonia. While you might not find hosts in Torres del Paine, larger towns like Punta Arenas or Bariloche have active Couchsurfing communities. It's not just free accommodation - it's a chance to see Patagonia through local eyes.

Lastly, don't overlook good old-fashioned guidebooks. The Lonely Planet Patagonia guide, for instance, often lists small, family-run hostels or tours that don't have a big online presence. It's like having a knowledgeable Patagonia expert in your backpack!

Remember, booking a trip to Patagonia isn't just about finding the cheapest deals. It's about crafting a journey that resonates with your travel style and connects you with the heart and soul of this incredible region. Whether you're clicking through online booking sites or scribbling down recommendations from fellow travelers in a Patagonian cafe, each booking is a step closer to the adventure of a lifetime.

So, fire up that laptop, dust off your passport, and get ready to book your way to Patagonian perfection. The glaciers are calling, the pumas are prowling, and a boat somewhere in Tierra del Fuego has a seat with your name on it. Buen viaje!

CHAPTER 2: MUST-SEE ATTRACTIONS AND LANDMARKS

Patagonia's breathtaking landscapes are a feast for the senses, offering everything from towering mountains to ancient cave art. The thunderous roar of Perito Moreno Glacier, the jagged peaks of Torres del Paine, and the challenging ascent of Fitz Roy Mountain all showcase nature's raw power and beauty. These iconic landmarks draw adventurers and nature lovers from around the world, promising unforgettable experiences and jaw-dropping vistas.

At the southern tip, Tierra del Fuego National Park feels like the edge of the world, while Península Valdés brings visitors face-to-face with amazing marine life. The ethereal Marble Caves and the ancient handprints of Cueva de las Manos offer glimpses into Patagonia's geological and human history. Meanwhile, Parque Nacional Nahuel Huapi's diverse ecosystems and the gravity-defying Queulat Hanging Glacier remind us of nature's incredible variety and resilience.

From the lush forests and crystal-clear lakes of Nahuel Huapi to the penguin-covered shores of Magdalena Island, Patagonia's landmarks tell a story of wild beauty and untamed wilderness. Each site offers its own unique charm, whether it's the thrill of spotting wildlife, the challenge of a difficult hike, or the quiet awe of standing before millennia-old art. Together, these incredible places create a tapestry of experiences that capture the heart and imagination of all who visit this remarkable corner of the world.

Perito Moreno Glacier

Imagine standing before a wall of ice so massive it dwarfs skyscrapers. That's the Perito Moreno Glacier for you - a colossal frozen river that'll make your heart skip a beat. This icy giant isn't just big; it's one of the few glaciers in the world that's actually growing!

Located in Los Glaciares National Park, Perito Moreno stretches an impressive 30 kilometers long and towers up to 70 meters above the water. But here's the kicker - it's constantly on the move. The glacier advances up to 2 meters per day, creaking and groaning as it inches forward. Talk about a slow-motion spectacle!

The real show, though, is when chunks of ice crash into the lake below. These "calving" events happen regularly, sending thunderous booms echoing across the landscape and creating mini tsunamis in the turquoise waters. It's nature's own drama, playing out right before your eyes.

But Perito Moreno isn't just about ice. The surrounding area is a wonderland of Andean-Patagonian forest, home to foxes, huemul deer, and if you're lucky, even pumas. Boardwalks allow you to get tantalizingly close to the glacier's face, offering different perspectives as you stroll along.

For the adventurous souls, you can actually trek on the glacier itself. Strap on some crampons, and suddenly you're walking on a landscape that looks more like the moon than Earth. Peer into deep blue crevasses, sip water from crystal-clear streams, and feel the ancient ice beneath your feet.

Interestingly, every few years, Perito Moreno puts on an even more spectacular show. The advancing ice creates a natural dam in Lago Argentino, causing water levels to rise dramatically on one side. Eventually, the pressure becomes too much, and the ice bridge collapses in a breathtaking display of nature's power. It's an event so rare and magnificent that people travel from all over the world just to witness it.

As the day progresses, the glacier's colors shift with the changing light. From stark white in the midday sun to soft pinks and purples at sunset, it's like watching a chameleon made of ice. And if you stick around after dark, you might even catch the glacier glowing under a canopy of Patagonian stars.

Perito Moreno isn't just a sight to see; it's a force of nature to experience. The sound of cracking ice, the crisp air on your face, the sheer scale of it all - it's a full sensory journey that'll stay with you long after you've left Patagonia behind. So come, stand in awe before this frozen giant, and let it remind you of the incredible, ever-changing world we live in.

Torres del Paine

Imagine a place where jagged peaks pierce cotton-candy clouds, turquoise lakes mirror the sky, and wild guanacos roam freely. Welcome to Torres del Paine, a slice of Patagonian paradise that'll make your heart race and your camera work overtime.

The park's crown jewels are the three granite towers that give it its name. These massive spires, sculpted by glaciers over millions of years, stand like sentinels watching over the landscape. At sunrise, they light up in shades of pink and gold, creating a natural light show that'll have you pinching yourself to make sure you're not dreaming.

But Torres del Paine isn't just about those famous peaks. The park is a patchwork of diverse ecosystems, from windswept pampas to dense lenga forests. One minute you're trekking through open grasslands, the next you're surrounded by gnarled trees draped in otherworldly lichens. It's like walking through different worlds in a single day.

Wildlife spotting here is a treat. Keep your eyes peeled for soaring condors, their massive wingspans casting shadows on the ground below. If you're lucky, you might spot the elusive puma prowling the hillsides, or catch a glimpse of the endangered huemul deer. And those fluffy creatures that look like llamas? Those are guanacos, distant cousins of camels that call this rugged landscape home.

The park's lakes and rivers are a whole other spectacle. Lake Pehoe's waters shift from deep blue to bright turquoise depending on the light, while the milky Grey Lake is dotted with icebergs that have broken off from the nearby glacier. Speaking of which, don't miss the chance to get up close to Grey Glacier. The sound of ancient ice creaking and popping is something you'll never forget.

For the adventurous, Torres del Paine offers some of the best hiking in South America. The famous W Trek takes you through the park's highlights over 4-5 days, while the full Circuit offers an even more immersive 7-10 day journey. But don't worry if long treks aren't your thing – there are plenty of day hikes and viewpoints accessible to all fitness levels.

One of the park's most unique features is its ever-changing weather. You might experience four seasons in a single day here. One moment you're basking in sunshine, the next you're battling sideways rain and howling winds. It's all part of the Torres del Paine experience, and it keeps things exciting!

As night falls, prepare for a celestial show like no other. The park's remote location and lack of light pollution make it perfect for stargazing. On clear nights, the Milky Way stretches across the sky, so vivid you'll feel like you could reach out and touch it.

Torres del Paine isn't just a national park; it's a reminder of the raw, untamed beauty our planet still holds. It's a place that challenges you, inspires you, and leaves you in awe of nature's artistry. So lace up your hiking boots, charge your camera batteries, and get ready for an adventure that'll stay with you for a lifetime.

Fitz Roy Mountain

Picture a mountain so striking, so perfectly sculpted, it inspired the logo for an entire outdoor clothing brand. That's Fitz Roy for you - a granite titan that beckons climbers and dreamers from across the globe.

Towering at 3,405 meters (11,171 feet), Fitz Roy isn't the tallest mountain in Patagonia, but it might just be the most charismatic. Its sheer granite faces rise abruptly from the surrounding landscape, creating a silhouette so distinctive you'd recognize it anywhere. The indigenous Tehuelche people called it Chaltén, meaning "smoking mountain," because its peak is often shrouded in clouds, giving the illusion of a volcano.

But here's the thing about Fitz Roy - it's notoriously moody. The weather here changes faster than a teenager's social media status. One minute you're basking in sunshine, the next you're engulfed in a sideways snowstorm. This fickle nature makes climbing Fitz Roy one of mountaineering's greatest challenges. In fact, it was considered one of the most difficult mountains in the world to climb until the 1950s.

The first ascent of Fitz Roy is the stuff of legend. In 1952, French alpinists Lionel Terray and Guido Magnone battled fierce storms and treacherous ice for weeks before finally reaching the summit. Today, climbers still speak of Fitz Roy with a mix of reverence and trepidation. Its routes have intimidating names like "Supercanaleta" and "The California Route," hinting at the adventures (and challenges) that await.

But don't worry if you're not into risking life and limb on vertical rock faces. Fitz Roy is just as captivating from ground level. The trek to its base is a Patagonian rite of passage, taking you through magical lenga forests and past crystal-clear alpine lakes. The view of the mountain reflected in Laguna de los Tres is the stuff postcards are made of - except no photo can quite capture the scale and majesty of seeing it in person.

Wildlife around Fitz Roy is as tough and resourceful as the mountain itself. Keep an eye out for condors riding the thermals, their massive wingspans making them look like prehistoric creatures. You might spot a shy huemul deer peeking out from the trees, or hear the distinctive call of the magellanic woodpecker echoing through the forest.

As the day progresses, Fitz Roy puts on a natural light show that'll leave you speechless. At sunrise, the eastern face glows a brilliant orange, earning it the nickname "The Fire Mountains." Come sunset, the granite takes on soft pinks and purples, Crafting a visually stunning scene that evokes a profound emotional reaction, leaving the observer mesmerized by its breathtaking beauty.

Here's a fun fact: Fitz Roy isn't just one peak, but part of a family. It's surrounded by other impressive spires like Aguja Poincenot and Cerro Torre, creating a skyline that looks like something out of a fantasy novel. Together, they form a natural amphitheater that'll make you feel tiny in the best possible way.

Whether you're a hardcore climber dreaming of conquering its summit, a hiker eager to reach its base, or simply someone who appreciates nature's artistry, Fitz Roy has something for everyone. It's more than just a mountain - it's a symbol of Patagonia's wild spirit, a test of human endurance, and a reminder of the awe-inspiring power of the natural world.

So come, let Fitz Roy work its magic on you. Just don't be surprised if you find yourself planning your return trip before you've even left.

Tierra del Fuego National Park

Welcome to the edge of the Earth! Tierra del Fuego National Park is where the South American continent makes its last dramatic stand before surrendering to the wild Southern Ocean. This is a land of extremes, where forests meet the sea, mountains plunge into icy waters, and the spirit of adventure is as palpable as the crisp Patagonian air.

Sprawling across 63,000 hectares, this park is a mix of rugged mountains, pristine lakes, and windswept beaches. It's the southernmost national park in the world, a title that comes with some pretty cool perks. During summer, you can experience the "midnight sun," with daylight stretching well past 10 PM. In winter, the park transforms into a snowy wonderland, perfect for cross-country skiing and spotting the elusive Magellanic woodpecker.

One of the park's most unique features is its "flag trees." These lenga beech trees have been shaped by relentless winds into natural works of art, their branches all pointing in one direction like wind-blown flags. It's nature's own version of a compass, pointing persistently eastward.

The park is home to some of the world's southernmost ecosystems. Here, you can walk through sub-Antarctic forests filled with lenga, coihue, and ñire trees, some of which are over 600 years old. These ancient woodlands are draped in mosses and lichens, creating an almost mystical atmosphere that feels like stepping into a fairy tale.

Wildlife here has adapted to the harsh conditions in fascinating ways. The Fuegian fox, found nowhere else on Earth, sports a thick, warm coat to weather the cold. Keen-eyed visitors might spot the elusive

Andean condor soaring overhead or catch a glimpse of the charming southern river otter playing in the park's many waterways.

Speaking of water, Tierra del Fuego is a paradise for kayakers and canoeists. Paddle along the Lapataia River, where the still waters perfectly mirror the surrounding mountains, creating a disorienting but beautiful effect. Or, if you're feeling brave, take a dip in Lago Roca – but be warned, it's chilly even in summer!

History buffs will love exploring the park's rich cultural heritage. The Yámana people lived here for thousands of years before European contact, developing ingenious ways to thrive in this challenging environment. Look out for ancient shell middens along the coast, silent testaments to their long presence in the region.

One of the park's most popular attractions is the "End of the World Train," a narrow-gauge railway that was originally built by prisoners of the nearby penal colony. Today, it offers a scenic ride through the park, complete with stops at a cascading waterfall and stunning viewpoints.

For hikers, the Costera Trail is a must-do. This coastal path takes you through ever-changing landscapes, from pebble beaches to dense forests, with the Beagle Channel as your constant companion. Keep an eye out for black-browed albatrosses and fur seals lounging on offshore islands.

As you explore, you might notice something peculiar – many of the park's plants are miniature versions of their northern cousins. It's an adaptation to the harsh climate, proving that even at the end of the world, life finds a way to thrive.

Tierra del Fuego National Park isn't just a place to visit; it's a place to experience. It's where you can stand at the very tip of a continent, breathe in the freshest air on Earth, and feel the exhilaration of being somewhere truly wild and remote. So come, add your footprints to the edge of the world, and let Tierra del Fuego work its magic on you.

Península Valdés

Imagine a place where massive elephant seals lounge on beaches, killer whales purposefully strand themselves to catch sea lion pups, and southern right whales perform aquatic ballets just offshore. Welcome to Península Valdés, a wildlife lover's dream come true!

This UNESCO World Heritage site juts out into the Atlantic Ocean like a giant thumbs-up, creating a natural sanctuary for an incredible array of marine life. It's one of the few places on Earth where you can witness such a diverse cast of animal characters without donning scuba gear.

The star of the show here is undoubtedly the southern right whale. These gentle giants visit the peninsula's sheltered bays from June to December, turning the waters into a real-life whale nursery. Mothers and calves often swim so close to shore you can hear their thunderous exhalations from the beach. Talk about a front-row seat to nature's greatest performance!

But the wildlife spectacle doesn't stop there. The peninsula is home to the largest breeding colony of elephant seals outside of Antarctica. These blubbery behemoths can weigh up to 4 tons – that's like a small car with whiskers! Watching the males battle for beach supremacy is like witnessing a sumo wrestling match in slow motion.

One of the peninsula's most unique attractions is its population of orcas. These crafty hunters have developed a one-of-a-kind hunting technique. During high tide, they'll partially beach themselves to snatch unsuspecting sea lion pups from the shallows. It's a risky maneuver that's rarely seen anywhere else in the world.

Birdwatchers, get your binoculars ready! Península Valdés is a feathered paradise. Magellanic penguins waddle along the shores, their tuxedo-like plumage a stark contrast to the golden sands. Keep an eye out for the impressive Andean condor – with a wingspan of up to 3.3 meters, these birds are like flying carpets with beaks!

The landscape here is as captivating as its inhabitants. The peninsula is a patchwork of wind-swept steppes, towering cliffs, and pristine beaches. Salt lakes dot the interior, their pink hues created by tiny algae. It's like Mother Nature decided to paint with her entire palette.

For the adventurous, kayaking along the coast offers a unique perspective. Paddle alongside curious sea lions or, if you're lucky, find yourself in the middle of a pod of playful dusky dolphins. Just remember, in these waters, you're the visitor in their aquatic living room!

History buffs will appreciate the peninsula's cultural significance. The indigenous Tehuelche people lived here for thousands of years, leaving behind artifacts and a rich oral tradition. Today, you can visit traditional Patagonian estancias (ranches) to get a taste of gaucho life and sample some of the best lamb you'll ever eat.

One of the peninsula's quirkiest residents is the Patagonian mara. This large rodent looks like a cross between a rabbit and a deer, hopping across the landscape on its long legs. It's just another example of the unique creatures that call this place home.

As day turns to night, the peninsula transforms. In the absence of light pollution, the night sky transforms into a captivating canvas for stargazing, offering a breathtaking display of celestial wonders.. On clear nights, the Milky Way stretches across the sky like a celestial highway, reminding you just how far from the beaten path you've ventured.

Península Valdés isn't just a destination; it's a front-row ticket to one of nature's greatest shows. It's a place where the line between land and sea blurs, where wild creatures reign supreme, and where every visit promises a new and awe-inspiring experience. So come, let the salty breeze tousle your hair, and prepare to be amazed by the wonders of this Patagonian paradise.

Marble Caves

Tucked away in the heart of Patagonia, the Marble Caves are like something straight out of a fantasy novel. Imagine swirling patterns of blue, turquoise, and gray, all reflected in crystal-clear waters. It's as if Mother Nature decided to try her hand at abstract art, using an entire cave system as her canvas.

These otherworldly caves are found on the shores of General Carrera Lake, which straddles the Chile-Argentina border. But don't let the name fool you – these caves aren't actually made of marble. They're solid limestone that's been shaped and painted by water over thousands of years. It's like the world's slowest, most beautiful erosion project.

The real magic of the Marble Caves lies in their ever-changing appearance. The colors you see depend on the water levels and the time of year. In spring, when the glacial melt is at its peak, the waters are a deep, sapphire blue. Come autumn, they shift to a mesmerizing turquoise. It's like the caves have their own mood ring!

Getting to the Marble Caves is an adventure in itself. The nearest town, Puerto Río Tranquilo, is a tiny settlement that feels like it's at the edge of the world. From there, you'll need to hop on a boat or kayak to reach the caves. As you approach, it's hard not to feel like you're entering a secret, hidden world.

One of the most famous formations in the cave system is called the "Marble Cathedral." This massive cavern features intricate swirls and patterns that'll make you wonder if you've stumbled into some underwater church. It's a place that seems to demand hushed voices and wide-eyed wonder.

For the adventurous souls, kayaking through the caves offers an unparalleled experience. Glide silently through turquoise waters, run your hand along the smooth, cool walls, and feel like you're exploring an alien planet. Just be prepared for some sore arms the next day – those paddles don't move themselves!

Here's a cool fact: the Marble Caves are actually the visible part of a much larger marble peninsula that extends deep underwater. It's like an iceberg – what you see is just the tip of a massive, hidden wonder.

Photography enthusiasts, bring all your gear (in waterproof bags, of course). The interplay of light, water, and stone creates endless opportunities for stunning shots. But fair warning: no photo can quite capture the magic of being there in person.

The caves have their own unique ecosystem. Look closely, and you might spot tiny fish darting through the clear waters or unusual plants clinging to the rock faces. It's a reminder that even in the most seemingly inhospitable places, life finds a way.

As you explore, keep in mind that these caves are incredibly fragile. The same water that created them is slowly wearing them away. Scientists estimate that in a few hundred years, they might disappear entirely. It's a sobering thought that makes the experience even more precious.

Visiting the Marble Caves isn't just a sightseeing trip – it's a journey to one of the planet's most unique and beautiful natural wonders. It's a place that reminds us of the incredible artistry of nature, the power of water to shape our world, and the importance of protecting these fragile ecosystems.

So come, float through these magical caverns, let your fingers trail in the cool, clear water, and lose yourself in the swirling patterns of stone. Just don't be surprised if you leave feeling like you've just woken up from the most beautiful dream.

Cueva de las Manos

Imagine a place where you can reach out and almost touch the fingerprints of our ancestors from 9,000 years ago. Welcome to Cueva de las Manos, or "Cave of Hands," a mind-blowing window into the distant past that'll make your jaw drop and your imagination run wild.

Tucked away in a remote canyon in Argentina's Santa Cruz province, this prehistoric art gallery showcases hundreds of colorful handprints splashed across the rock face. But these aren't just any handprints – they're negative images created by ancient artists blowing pigment through hollow bones around their hands. It's like prehistoric spray painting!

The sheer number of hands is staggering – over 800 in total. Most are left hands, leading archaeologists to believe the artists held their 'spray cans' in their right hands. But here's a cool twist: some of the hands are tiny, belonging to children. Imagine a Stone Age family outing, kids leaving their mark alongside their parents!

The colors used in the cave paintings are still vibrant after thousands of years, ranging from red and orange to black. The pigments were made from natural materials like iron oxides, kaolin, and natrojarosite. It's like these ancient artists found nature's own paint set and went to town.

But it's not just hands that grace these walls. The cave also features incredible depictions of guanacos (a wild llama relative), rheas (like ostriches), and hunting scenes. One famous image shows a group of hunters surrounding a guanaco – it's an ancient action movie frozen in time.

Here's a mind-bending fact: the oldest paintings in the cave date back to around 7300 BC. That's older than the pyramids, older than Stonehenge, older than writing itself. When you stand in this cave, you're literally looking at one of the oldest examples of human artistic expression on the planet.

The cave itself is no small feat to reach. It's nestled in the valley of the Pinturas River, surrounded by stark, beautiful Patagonian landscape. The journey there feels like traveling back in time, away from the modern world and into a land where nature and ancient human history intertwine.

Archaeologists have learned a ton from studying these paintings. They've figured out that the people who made them were nomadic hunter-gatherers, following guanaco herds across the Patagonian plains. The cave was likely a special place, maybe used for ceremonies or as a kind of prehistoric message board.

One of the coolest things about Cueva de las Manos is how it brings our ancient ancestors to life. These weren't just primitive cavemen – they were artists, storytellers, and innovators. They figured out how to make paint last for millennia and developed techniques to create these haunting images.

Visiting the cave today is a powerful experience. As you stand there, surrounded by these ancient handprints, it's hard not to feel a connection to the people who made them. You might find yourself holding up your own hand, comparing it to those on the wall, bridging a gap of thousands of years with a simple gesture.

Cueva de las Manos isn't just an archaeological site – it's a reminder of our shared human heritage. It shows us that the urge to create, to leave our mark on the world, is as old as humanity itself. So come, stand in the footsteps of our ancestors, and add your own story to the ongoing human tale that began in this remarkable cave so long ago.

Parque Nacional Nahuel Huapi

Picture a place where crystal-clear lakes mirror snow-capped peaks, where lush forests hide secret waterfalls, and where you might just bump into a pudú – the world's smallest deer. Welcome to Parque Nacional Nahuel Huapi, Argentina's oldest national park and a playground for nature lovers and adventure seekers alike.

Sprawling across a whopping 7,050 square kilometers, this park is like a greatest hits album of Patagonian landscapes. At its heart lies the massive Lake Nahuel Huapi, shaped like a giant octopus with tentacle-like fingers reaching into the surrounding valleys. The Mapuche people named it "Island of the Jaguar," though you're more likely to spot a river otter than a big cat these days.

One of the park's coolest features is its incredible biodiversity. You can start your day in arid steppe, hike through temperate rainforest dripping with ferns and moss, and end up in alpine tundra – all without leaving the park boundaries. It's like traveling through different climate zones without needing a passport!

Towering over it all is Mount Tronador, an extinct volcano straddling the Chile-Argentina border. Its name means "Thunderer" in Spanish, thanks to the booming sound of falling seracs (ice towers) from its glaciers. Speaking of which, don't miss the Black Glacier – its dark color comes from accumulated volcanic ash, making it look like nature's own chocolate ice cream.

For the adventurous, Nahuel Huapi is a veritable buffet of outdoor activities. Hike the challenging Cerro Catedral for panoramic views that'll make your Instagram followers drool. Kayak the mirror-like waters of Lake Mascardi, or try your hand at fly-fishing in one of the park's many rivers. In winter, strap on your skis and hit the slopes at Cerro Catedral, South America's largest ski resort.

History buffs, listen up! The park has some fascinating stories to tell. It was here that Francisco Moreno, the "Perito" (expert) who helped settle Argentina's border disputes, donated the initial land for the park. You can visit his log cabin, now a museum, on Centenary Island in Lake Nahuel Huapi.

One of the park's quirkiest residents is the Monito del Monte, or "Little Monkey of the Mountain." Don't let the name fool you – it's actually a tiny marsupial, a living fossil related to Australian possums. Spotting one of these nocturnal cuties is like winning the wildlife lottery!

Nahuel Huapi is also home to some seriously old trees. The alerce forests in the park include specimens over 3,000 years old. Standing next to these ancient giants, you can't help but feel a sense of awe – and maybe a little young in comparison.

For a touch of luxury in the wilderness, check out Llao Llao Hotel. This iconic lodge looks like it was plucked from a European fairytale and plonked down in the middle of Patagonia. Even if you're not staying there, it's worth a visit for the stunning views and a taste of old-world glamour.

Don't miss the chance to sail to Victoria Island, where you can wander through forests of transplanted trees from around the world. It's like a global arboretum in the middle of a Patagonian lake – talk about unexpected!

As night falls, the park transforms. On clear nights, the lack of light pollution turns the sky into a glittering canvas of stars. If you're lucky, you might even catch the ethereal glow of the Southern Lights dancing across the horizon.

Parque Nacional Nahuel Huapi isn't just a place to visit – it's a place to experience with all your senses. Feel the crisp mountain air on your face, listen to the thunderous roar of waterfalls, taste the sweet wild berries (if your guide says they're safe!), and let the sheer beauty of this Patagonian wonderland seep into your soul. Just be prepared – you might find yourself planning your return trip before you've even left!

Queulat Hanging Glacier

Imagine a massive tongue of ice clinging to a sheer cliff face, defying gravity and logic. That's the Queulat Hanging Glacier for you – a frozen marvel that'll make you question everything you thought you knew about glaciers.

Tucked away in Chile's Queulat National Park, this icy wonder looks like it's been caught mid-fall, frozen in time. It's not just hanging there for show, though. The glacier regularly calves chunks of ice that crash down the cliff, creating a natural ice fountain that feeds the milky-turquoise lake below. It's like watching the world's slowest, coldest waterfall in action.

Reaching the glacier presents a thrilling adventure in its own right.. The journey takes you along the infamous Carretera Austral, a road that winds through some of Patagonia's most untamed wilderness. As you approach the park, you'll find yourself in a valley so lush and green it feels more like a rainforest than the home of a glacier. This unique microclimate is part of what makes Queulat so special – where else can you see tropical-looking ferns growing just a stone's throw from ancient ice?

The best view of the glacier comes at the end of a moderate hike through the Bosque Encantado (Enchanted Forest). As you trek through moss-draped trees and over gurgling streams, you'll feel like you've stepped into a fairytale. Then, suddenly, the trees part and – bam! – there's the glacier, hanging impossibly between mountain peaks. It's a view that'll stop you in your tracks and have you fumbling for your camera.

Here's a cool fact: the Queulat Hanging Glacier is actually a remnant of the Patagonian Ice Sheet that covered much of southern Chile and Argentina during the last ice age. It's like a window into Earth's prehistoric past, right there in front of you.

For the more adventurous, kayaking on the lagoon below the glacier offers a unique perspective. Paddle through icy waters, dodging mini-icebergs, with the glacier looming above you. Just be prepared for a chilly experience – that water is seriously cold!

Birdwatchers, keep your eyes peeled. The park is home to some fascinating feathered friends, including the Magellanic woodpecker with its distinctive red head, and the Chilean pigeon, found nowhere else on Earth. It's like a real-life game of Pokémon – gotta spot 'em all!

One of the most magical times to visit is early morning when mist often shrouds the valley. As the sun rises and burns off the fog, it's like watching the glacier emerge from the clouds – a real-life reveal worthy of any nature documentary.

The area around Queulat is also known for its hot springs. After a day of hiking and glacier-gazing, there's nothing quite like soaking in naturally heated waters while surrounded by pristine wilderness. It's nature's own spa treatment.

Here's something to ponder as you gaze at the glacier: it's changing. Like many glaciers worldwide, Queulat is retreating due to climate change. Visiting isn't just about seeing a natural wonder – it's about witnessing a landscape in flux, a reminder of our planet's delicate balance.

As day turns to night, the glacier takes on a new persona. If you're lucky enough to visit on a full moon, you might see the ice glowing an ethereal blue in the moonlight. It's a sight that'll make you feel like you've stepped onto another planet.

Queulat Hanging Glacier isn't just a sight to see – it's a full sensory experience. The crisp air on your face, the rumble of distant ice falls, the play of light on ancient ice – it all comes together to create a moment of pure Patagonian magic. So come, stand in awe before this frozen giant, and let it remind you of the incredible, ever-changing world we live in. Just don't forget to pick your jaw up off the ground when you're done!

Magdalena Island

Imagine an island where penguins outnumber people by about 60,000 to 1. Welcome to Magdalena Island, a pint-sized chunk of land in the Strait of Magellan that's become one of nature's most adorable penguin colonies.

Just a stone's throw from Punta Arenas, this tiny island packs a big wildlife punch. It's home to over 120,000 Magellanic penguins, who waddle around like they own the place (which, let's face it, they kinda do). These tuxedo-clad birds come here every year between September and March to breed, molt, and generally live their best penguin lives.

Getting to Magdalena is half the fun. A two-hour boat ride takes you through the legendary Strait of Magellan, where you might spot dolphins, sea lions, and even the occasional whale. As you approach the island, you'll see what looks like a moving carpet of black and white – yep, those are all penguins!

Once on the island, you'll follow a marked path that winds through the penguin colony. But here's the kicker – the penguins have zero respect for human boundaries. Don't be surprised if you find yourself doing a penguin shuffle to avoid tripping over these curious little guys as they cross the path.

The island's lighthouse, built in 1902, stands tall amidst the penguin chaos. Climb to the top for a bird's eye view of the colony – it's like looking down on a living, breathing game of chess.

Magdalena Island isn't just about penguins, though. It's a crucial nesting site for other seabirds too. Keep an eye out for cormorants, austral seagulls, and Antarctic pigeons. It's like a feathered United Nations down here!

Here's a fun fact: Magellanic penguins are monogamous and return to the same partner and nest each year. As you walk around, you might spot penguin couples engaged in what looks like bill fencing – it's actually their way of saying "Hey, honey, I'm home!"

The island holds several unexpected discoveries in store. Hidden among the penguin burrows are the remains of ancient Kawéskar settlements. These indigenous people once used the island as a stopover on their canoe journeys. It's a poignant reminder of the human history intertwined with this natural wonderland.

Visiting Magdalena requires some careful timing. The island is only open to visitors during the penguin breeding season, and even then, bad weather can cancel trips at the last minute. But trust me, when you're standing in the middle of a sea of penguins, you'll know it was worth the wait.

One of the coolest things about Magdalena is how close you can get to the penguins. But remember, no touching! These little guys might look cuddly, but they're wild animals and need their space. Plus, those beaks are sharper than they look!

As you explore, keep an ear out for the unique braying call of the Magellanic penguin. It sounds a bit like a donkey with a sore throat, but to penguin ears, it's a sweet melody.

The island plays a crucial role in penguin conservation. Researchers regularly visit to monitor the population and health of the colony. Your visit actually helps support these efforts – ecotourism at its finest!

As your time on Magdalena comes to an end, you might find yourself not wanting to leave. There's something magical about being surrounded by thousands of these charming, waddling birds. It's a reminder of the incredible diversity of life on our planet and the importance of protecting these unique habitats.

So come, join the penguin party on Magdalena Island. Just don't be surprised if you leave with a newfound appreciation for black and white fashion and a strange urge to eat fish. After all, you've just spent a day in one of nature's most adorable wildlife sanctuaries!

CHAPTER 3: ACCOMMODATION OPTIONS

Patagonia's accommodation scene is as diverse as its landscapes, offering something for every traveler and budget. From luxurious lodges nestled in the Andes to cozy hostels in charming towns, you'll find a place to rest your head after a day of adventure. Whether you're looking to splurge on a high-end resort with breathtaking views or save your pesos for experiences by opting for budget-friendly digs, Patagonia has you covered.

For those seeking a truly unique stay, the region boasts an array of unconventional options. Imagine waking up in a dome with a view of Torres del Paine or spending the night in a traditional estancia. These local favorites not only provide a comfortable bed but also immerse you in the Patagonian way of life. And if you're feeling overwhelmed by the choices, don't worry - a little planning goes a long way in securing the perfect accommodation.

When booking your Patagonian home away from home, keep in mind that popular spots fill up quickly during peak season. It's wise to book well in advance, especially for those bucket-list locations. Also, consider the proximity to your planned activities and the amenities that matter most to you. With a bit of research and some insider tips, you'll find the ideal base for your Patagonian adventure, whether it's a luxury spa resort or a cheerful backpacker hostel.

Best Luxury Hotels and Resorts

Patagonia's Lap of Luxury: Where Wilderness Meets Opulence

Picture this: You've just conquered the rugged trails of Torres del Paine, your muscles ache, and your soul is brimming with the raw beauty of Patagonia. Now, imagine sinking into a plush bed, gazing at snow-capped peaks through floor-to-ceiling windows, while a sommelier uncorks a bottle of Malbec. Welcome to Patagonia's luxury accommodations, where wild adventure meets world-class pampering.

Let's start our indulgent journey at The Singular Patagonia, a converted cold storage plant turned five-star hotel in Puerto Bories. This architectural marvel blends industrial chic with sumptuous comfort. Don't miss their spa's glacial water therapies trust me, your tired limbs will thank you. And the restaurant? It's a culinary love letter to Patagonian flavors. Try the king crab risotto; it's a game-changer.

For those who crave isolation (in style, of course), Awasi Patagonia is your ticket to privacy. Each of its 14 villas comes with a private guide and 4WD vehicle. Fancy a midnight trek to spot pumas? Your wish is their command. The best part? Your villa's outdoor hot tub, perfect for stargazing while sipping on a pisco sour.

If you're all about those postcard-perfect views, Explora Patagonia in Torres del Paine National Park is your holy grail. Perched on the shores of Lake Pehoé, it offers front-row seats to the iconic Paine Massif. Their all-inclusive program means you can focus on choosing between horseback riding, hiking, or simply lounging by the infinity pool (no judgment here).

For a touch of Relais & Châteaux elegance, head to Eolo in El Calafate. This sprawling 10,000-acre estancia seamlessly blends into the Patagonian steppe. Their farm-to-table restaurant is a gastronomic journey through the region. Pro tip: Book a room facing La Anita Valley for sunrise views that'll make you question if you're still on Earth.

Now, if you're a wine enthusiast (and let's be honest, who isn't?), Casa de Uco in the Uco Valley is your slice of heaven. This working vineyard and luxury resort offers wine-infused spa treatments, private asados (Argentine barbecues), and the chance to blend your own wine. Imagine sipping your personal creation while watching the sun set over the Andes. Pure bliss.

Last but not least, for those who want to literally sleep under the stars, Patagonia Camp's luxury yurts are calling your name. These circular tents come with skylights for aurora-spotting and heating for those chilly Patagonian nights. It's glamping at its finest, complete with a gourmet restaurant and a view of the Paine Massif that'll make your Instagram followers green with envy.

luxury in Patagonia isn't just about thread counts and Michelin stars. It's about experiencing this wild frontier in comfort and style, with experiences tailored to your wildest dreams. So go ahead, treat yourself. After all, you've earned it trekking through one of the world's last great wildernesses.

Budget-Friendly Accommodations

Patagonia on a Shoestring: Where Adventure Meets Affordability

Think experiencing Patagonia's breathtaking beauty is reserved for the deep-pocketed? Think again! This wild frontier isn't just for luxury seekers. With a bit of savvy planning, you can explore this awe-inspiring region without breaking the bank. Let's dive into Patagonia's budget-friendly accommodation scene, where the views are million-dollar, but the price tags aren't.

First stop: El Chaltén, Argentina's hiking paradise. Here, you'll find America del Sur Hostel, a backpacker's dream come true. Picture yourself swapping trail stories around a roaring fire, guitar strumming in the background, with a view of Mount Fitz Roy that'll make you pinch yourself. Their communal kitchen is a melting pot of cultures and cuisines – whip up some trail mix alongside a French pastry chef or an Aussie surfer. Pro tip: Book their weekly asado night for a taste of authentic Argentine barbecue that won't dent your wallet.

Heading to Torres del Paine? Check out Refugio Paine Grande. This no-frills mountain hut is your ticket to experiencing the park's heart without the hefty price tag. Sure, you might be bunking with fellow trekkers, but nothing beats the camaraderie of sharing instant noodles after a day conquering the trails. Plus, waking up to the Torres at your doorstep? Priceless.

In Punta Arenas, the Hospedaje Costanera is a hidden gem. This family-run guesthouse feels more like crashing at your long-lost Chilean aunt's place. Doña María's homemade sopaipillas (fried pastries) at breakfast will fuel you for a day of penguin-spotting. The best part? The owners are a treasure trove of local knowledge, pointing you to off-the-beaten-path spots that guidebooks miss.

For a uniquely Patagonian experience that won't break the bank, try La Guanaca Hostel in Puerto Natales. This converted estancia (ranch) lets you live out your gaucho fantasies without the luxury price tag. Learn to lasso, help herd sheep, or simply chill in a hammock under the vast Patagonian sky. Their "mate andmedialuna" afternoons are a crash course in Argentine culture – just don't expect to sleep after all that caffeine!

In Ushuaia, "the End of the World," bunk down at Antarctica Hostel. Despite the name, it's surprisingly cozy. Their "prisoner's breakfast" (a nod to Ushuaia's history as a penal colony) is hearty enough to prep you for a day of exploring Tierra del Fuego National Park. Bonus: They offer free bikes, perfect for cruising along the Beagle Channel at sunset.

For those venturing to the Chilean side, Hospedaje Nordenskjöld in Puerto Varas is a steal. This charming wooden house offers lake views that'll make you question if you've stumbled into a postcard. The owners, an adorable elderly couple, treat guests like family. Don't be surprised if you're roped into an impromptu Spanish lesson over homemade kuchen (German-style cake, a nod to the area's immigrant history).

Remember, budget travel in Patagonia isn't just about pinching pennies it's about rich experiences, authentic connections, and the thrill of stretching your peso further. So lace up those hiking boots, pack that well-worn backpack, and get ready to experience Patagonia's magic, one affordable bunk at a time. After all, the best things in Patagonia – like that first glimpse of a calving glacier or the taste of mate shared with new friends – are absolutely free.

Unique Stays and Local Favorites

Quirky Quarters: Patagonia's Most Unforgettable Stays

Forget cookie-cutter hotel rooms. In Patagonia, your accommodation can be as wild and wonderful as the landscape itself. From cozy shepherd's huts to transparent bubble domes, these unique stays will have you questioning if you've stumbled into a fairy tale or a sci-fi flick.

To begin our exploration, let us embark on a journey to EcoCamp Patagonia, located within the breathtaking Torres del Paine National Park. Imagine snuggling up in a geodesic dome, designed to withstand Patagonia's infamous winds, with a skylight perfect for stargazing. It's like camping, but with proper beds and hot showers. Their community domes are social hubs where you can swap hiking tales over a glass of Carménère. But the real magic? Waking up to the Torres bathed in dawn's rosy light, right from your bed.

For a slice of history, bunk down at Estancia Harberton near Ushuaia. This sheep farm, Tierra del Fuego's oldest, was founded in 1886 by Anglican missionary Thomas Bridges. Stay in the original family home and you might find yourself chatting with Bridges' descendants over mate. Don't miss their on-site museum showcasing the area's rich marine life – it's a hidden gem that most tourists overlook.

Craving something truly off-grid? Head to Refugio Frey in Bariloche. This remote mountain hut, accessible only by a challenging hike, offers basic bunks and unforgettable views. Gather around the wood stove with climbers from around the world, sharing trail mix and tall tales. Fair warning: the outhouse trip at night is an adventure in itself!

For a taste of gaucho life, saddle up at Estancia Nibepo Aike in Los Glaciares National Park. This working ranch lets you channel your inner cowboy, from horseback riding to sheep shearing. The simple rooms in the original farmhouse ooze rustic charm. Don't miss their traditional asado, where you'll learn the art of Argentine barbecue from the experts.

Now, for something completely different: Patagonia Dome City in Chile's Aysén Region. These futuristic pods perched on stilts offer 360-degree views of the surrounding wilderness. It's like sleeping in a snow globe, minus the snow (usually). Their "dome spa" takes glamping to a whole new level – imagine soaking in a hot tub under the Southern Cross.

If you're all about location, location, location, book a night at Refugio Paine Grande. This basic but comfortable mountain hut sits smack in the middle of the W Trek in Torres del Paine. It's a hiker's dream – no frills, just pure Patagonian wilderness at your doorstep. Pro tip: pack earplugs. The communal dorms can get a bit, let's say, symphonic with snoring.

For a maritime adventure, why not spend a night aboard the Capitan Constantino? This refurbished cargo ship, moored in Puerto Natales, offers cozy cabins with porthole views. Fall asleep to the gentle lapping of waves and wake up to the call of cormorants. Their deck is the perfect spot for sundowners with a view of the Última Esperanza Sound.

Lastly, for those who like their accommodations with a side of adrenaline, check out Las Águilas Hotel in El Calafate. Here, the concept of "room with a view" is elevated to new and literal dimensions.

Their "nidos" (nests) are suspended pods hanging off a cliff face. It's not for the faint-hearted, but the bragging rights are off the charts.

Remember, in Patagonia, where you lay your head is part of the adventure. These unique stays aren't just places to sleep – they're gateways to experiencing the region's soul, its history, and its wild spirit. So go ahead, book that shepherd's hut or that suspended pod. After all, ordinary hotels are for ordinary vacations, and there's nothing ordinary about Patagonia.

Practical Tips for Booking Accommodations

Navigating Patagonia's Accommodation Scene: Insider Tips and Tricks

Alright, adventurers, let's talk booking strategy. Securing the perfect Patagonian pad isn't just about clicking "reserve" – it's an art form. With these insider tips, you'll be sleeping soundly in your dream digs, whether that's a luxury lodge or a rustic refugio.

First things first: timing is everything. Patagonia's peak season runs from December to February, when prices skyrocket faster than a condor on an updraft. Want to save some serious pesos? Aim for the shoulder seasons – October to November or March to April. You'll dodge the crowds, snag better deals, and still catch decent weather. Plus, autumn in Patagonia? It's a technicolor dream you won't want to miss.

Now, let's talk location. In Patagonia, it's not just about where you stay, but what you're staying for. Hiking the W Trek in Torres del Paine? Book refugios well in advance – they fill up faster than you can say "glacial moraine." Pro tip: some refugios offer "full board" options. It might seem pricey, but when you're exhausted from trekking, you'll thank yourself for not having to cook.

For the budget-savvy, consider basing yourself in hub towns like Puerto Natales or El Calafate. You'll find a wider range of affordable options, and day trips are easy to arrange. Bonus: you'll get a taste of local life beyond the tourist spots.

Speaking of local life, don't overlook homestays. Websites like Airbnb aren't just for city apartments – you can find some real gems in Patagonia. Imagine staying with a local family in Chaltén, getting insider tips on the best trails and learning to make authentic empanadas. It's cultural immersion and cozy accommodation rolled into one.

Now, a word on amenities. Patagonia isn't known for its high-speed Wi-Fi or 24/7 room service. Embrace it! But if you absolutely need to stay connected (we get it, those glacier pics won't post themselves), check the amenities list carefully. Many remote lodges rely on satellite internet, which can be... let's say, temperamental.

Here's a hot tip: look for accommodations with drying rooms or laundry facilities. Patagonian weather is as changeable as a chameleon on a disco floor. You'll appreciate being able to dry your gear after an unexpected downpour.

For the eco-conscious traveler (and in Patagonia, that should be everyone), seek out lodgings with sustainability credentials. Many places are leading the charge in green tourism, from solar-powered eco-lodges to estancias practicing regenerative agriculture. Your stay could actually help preserve this pristine wilderness.

If you're planning a multi-stop Patagonian odyssey, consider booking through a local agency. They often have relationships with properties across the region and can snag you better rates and perks. Plus, they're invaluable if you need to make last-minute changes – because in Patagonia, sometimes the wind has other plans.

Lastly, don't forget to check the cancellation policies. Patagonia's remoteness means getting there can sometimes be... adventurous. Look for flexible booking options, just in case that once-in-a-lifetime storm decides to hit during your travel dates.

Remember, in Patagonia, your accommodation is more than just a place to crash. It's part of the experience, a basecamp for adventure, and sometimes, an adventure in itself. So whether you're cozying up in a mountain refugio or living it up in a luxury lodge, embrace the Patagonian spirit. After all, the best stories often start with "You'll never believe where we stayed..."

CHAPTER 4: DINING AND CUISINE

Patagonia's culinary scene is a feast for the senses, blending rugged wilderness with refined flavors. From cozy family-run eateries serving up hearty stews to upscale restaurants plating gourmet creations, there's something to satisfy every palate. The region's best dining spots not only tantalize your taste buds but often come with a side of breathtaking views, whether it's snow-capped peaks or vast pampas stretching to the horizon.

Local flavors are the stars of Patagonian cuisine, with must-try dishes that reflect the land's bounty. Sink your teeth into succulent Patagonian lamb, savor the delicate taste of king crab, or warm up with a bowl of calafate berry soup. These regional specialties tell the story of Patagonia on a plate, often enjoyed in settings that'll make you want to linger long after dessert.

When dining out in Patagonia, embrace the relaxed pace and local customs. Don't be surprised if dinner starts late - it's all part of the experience. Sharing mate with new friends or learning the art of asado are more than just meals; they're cultural exchanges. Remember, in Patagonia, dining isn't just about food - it's about connection, to the land, its people, and the incredible flavors they create together.

Best Restaurants and Eateries

Patagonia's Culinary Gems: Where Flavor Meets Adventure

Forget what you've heard about Patagonia being all about rugged landscapes and outdoor thrills. This wild corner of the world is cooking up a storm, and trust me, your taste buds are in for the ride of their life!

Let's kick things off in El Calafate with La Tablita. This place is an institution, folks. It's been serving up sizzling steaks since before Perito Moreno Glacier was cool (okay, maybe not that long, but you get the idea). Their lamb al asador is so tender, it practically falls off the bone with a stern look. Pro tip: save room for the calafate berry mousse. Legend has it that eating these berries ensures your return to Patagonia. Who are we to argue with delicious superstition?

Now, if you find yourself in Ushuaia craving seafood (and let's be honest, who doesn't at the "End of the World"?), make a beeline for Kaupé. Perched on a hill overlooking the Beagle Channel, this place serves up king crab that'll make you question every other seafood experience you've ever had. Their chef, Ernesto, is a bit of a local celebrity. Rumor has it he once cooked for the crew of a stranded Antarctic expedition ship. Talk about pressure in the kitchen!

For those exploring the Chilean side, don't miss Afrigonia in Puerto Natales. This fusion restaurant is where Patagonian ingredients meet African cooking techniques. Sounds weird? Trust me, it works. Their guanaco carpaccio with maqui berry sauce is a flavor explosion that'll have you reconsidering everything you thought you knew about Patagonian cuisine.

Bariloche, Argentina's chocolate capital, is home to Butterfly. This restaurant offers not just a meal, but an evocative sensory experience. Chef Mariela Sammartino changes her menu with the seasons, using ingredients foraged from the surrounding Andean forests. Ever tried venison with wild mushrooms and Patagonian pine nuts? You're in for a treat.

For a truly unique dining experience, book a table at El Baqueano in El Chaltén. This tiny spot (seriously, it seats like 20 people max) is run by a husband-wife duo who forage for ingredients daily. Their tasting menu is a love letter to Patagonian flavors. The catch? The menu changes nightly based on what they find. It's like culinary roulette, and every spin is delicious.

If you're all about that farm-to-table life, Estancia Alice in Tierra del Fuego is your jam. This working sheep ranch lets you experience gaucho-style barbecue in all its glory. Watch as whole lambs are slow-roasted on iron crosses around an open fire. It's dinner and a show, Patagonian style.

For the plant-based crowd, fear not! Sativa in Punta Arenas is proving that vegan food can thrive even in the land of lamb and asado. Their lentil and mushroom "no-meat" balls would fool even the most dedicated carnivore. Plus, their hot chocolate (made with Patagonian water, of course) is like a warm hug on a cold day.

Last but not least, for those nights when you just can't deal with another fancy meal, hit up La Anónima in... well, pretty much any Patagonian town. This supermarket chain has a hot food section that locals swear by. Grab some empanadas, a slice of torta galesa (Welsh cake, a nod to

Patagonia's Welsh settlers), and have yourself a picnic under the Southern Cross.

Remember, eating in Patagonia isn't just about the food – it's about the stories, the people, and the incredible landscapes that inspire these culinary creations. So loosen that belt, bring your sense of adventure, and get ready to eat your way through one of the world's last great wildernesses. Buen provecho!

Local Flavors and Must-Try Dishes

Tastes of the Wild South: Patagonia's Flavor Fiesta

Alright, food lovers, buckle up! We're about to take your taste buds on a wild ride through Patagonia's culinary landscape. Forget what you think you know about South American food – this is a whole different ballgame.

Let's start with the star of the show: Patagonian lamb. These woolly wonders roam free on the vast steppes, munching on wild herbs and grasses. The result? Meat so flavorful, it'll make you want to hug a sheep (don't, though – they're not into it). Traditionally slow-roasted on a spit over an open fire, it's the centerpiece of any proper Patagonian asado. The crispy skin and melt-in-your-mouth meat are basically a religious experience.

Now, let's talk about something you probably didn't expect to find in Patagonia: king crab. Yep, you heard that right. The cold waters of the Beagle Channel are teeming with these massive crustaceans. Locals love them in chupe de centolla, a hearty crab stew that'll warm you up faster than you can say "brrr." It's like a hug in a bowl, with chunks of crab meat swimming in a creamy, cheesy broth.

For the adventurous eaters, how about some guanaco? These llama-like creatures are native to Patagonia, and their lean meat is starting to show up on menus across the region. Try it in a guanaco carpaccio, thinly sliced and drizzled with olive oil and local herbs. It's like beef, but with a wilder, gamier flavor that screams "I'm eating Patagonia!"

Got a sweet tooth? Meet the calafate berry. This tiny purple fruit is everywhere in Patagonia, and locals use it in everything from jams to cocktails. Legend has it that if you eat calafate, you're destined to return to Patagonia. Sounds like a good excuse for seconds to me! Try it in a calafate sour, a twist on the classic pisco sour that'll have you planning your next Patagonian adventure before you've even finished your drink.

Now, let's talk about something that might raise a few eyebrows: ostrich. Yep, these big birds are farmed in Patagonia, and their meat is lean, tender, and packed with flavor. Ostrich milanesa (think chicken-fried steak, but way cooler) is a local favorite that'll make you wonder why we don't eat more ostrich back home.

For a quick snack on the go, you can't beat a Patagonian empanada. These handheld pockets of joy come stuffed with everything from lamb to seafood. But the real MVP is the cordero al palo empanada – all the flavors of a traditional lamb roast, wrapped up in a flaky pastry. It's like carrying a whole asado in your pocket!

Vegetarians, don't feel left out! Patagonia's got you covered with chochoca, a Native Mapuche dish made from potato and wheat flour. It's often served as a savory pancake filled with wild mushrooms or native herbs. It's comfort food with a side of cultural heritage.

And let's not forget about Patagonia's liquid gold: mate. This caffeine-packed herbal tea is more than just a drink – it's a social ritual. Sharing mate with locals is a surefire way to make friends and maybe even pick up some Spanish slang.

Last but not least, wash it all down with a glass of Patagonian wine. The region's extreme climate produces some seriously interesting vinos. Try a Pinot Noir from the Chubut Valley – its complex, earthy notes are like Patagonia in a glass.

Eating in Patagonia isn't just about filling your belly – it's about connecting with the land, its people, and centuries of culinary tradition. So go ahead, be brave, and order that thing you can't pronounce. Your taste buds will thank you, and you'll have some great stories to take home (along with a few extra pounds, probably). ¡Buen provecho!

Dining with a View

Feast Your Eyes: Patagonia's Most Jaw-Dropping Dining Spots

Imagine this: You're fork-deep in a juicy steak, a glass of Malbec in hand, and suddenly you look up to see a glacier calving right before your eyes. Welcome to dining in Patagonia, where the views are as mouth watering as the food!

Let's start our scenic eating tour at Lago Grey Hotel's restaurant in Torres del Paine. Here, floor-to-ceiling windows offer a front-row seat to the Grey Glacier. As you tuck into your king crab risotto, you might spot electric blue icebergs floating by. It's like dinner and a show, courtesy of Mother Nature herself.

For a meal that'll really give you a bird's eye view, head to La Cucina in Ushuaia. Perched atop Martial Mountain, this cozy spot serves up homemade pasta with a side of panoramic vistas over the Beagle Channel. On a clear day, you can see all the way to Cape Horn. Just be careful not to drop your fork while gawking at the view – it's a long way down!

Now, if you're all about that gaucho life, saddle up and ride to Nibepo Aike in Los Glaciares National Park. This working estancia offers an authentic Patagonian asado experience. Picture this: you're chowing down on lamb fresh off the spit, the scent of wild herbs in the air, with the jagged peaks of Mount Fitz Roy as your backdrop. It's enough to make you want to trade in your day job for a life on the range.

For a dining experience that's literally on the move, book a spot on The Old Patagonian Express. This restored steam train chugs through the

Patagonian steppe while you enjoy a gourmet meal in the dining car. The menu changes with the seasons, but the view of the endless pampas rolling by is always on offer. It's like stepping back in time, with better food.

If you're more of a water baby, set sail for Pia Glacier in the Beagle Channel. Several cruise companies offer glacier-view lunches where you can munch on local delicacies while watching massive ice chunks tumble into the sea. The thunderous crack of calving ice is nature's version of a dinner bell.

For those who like their meals with a side of adrenaline, try lunch at Cerro Catedral ski resort near Bariloche. Ride the cable car up to La Roca restaurant, where you can refuel on hearty mountain fare while watching daredevil skiers tackle the slopes below. In summer, the view of Lake Nahuel Huapi stretching out beneath you is so stunning, you might forget to eat.

Now, let's talk about El Chalten, Argentina's trekking capital. After a long day on the trails, drag your tired feet to La Tapera. This rustic spot has a back patio with unobstructed views of Fitz Roy and Cerro Torre. As the alpenglow paints the peaks pink at sunset, you'll swear your craft beer tastes even better.

For a truly unique viewpoint, check out Bahia Paraiso in Puerto Natales. This restaurant is housed in a grounded ship with porthole windows looking out over Last Hope Sound. Dive into some fresh seafood while imagining the maritime adventures this old vessel must have seen.

Last but not least, for those nights when you just want to grab a quick bite, head to any local grocery store, stock up on cheese, bread, and wine, and have yourself a DIY picnic. Find a quiet spot overlooking a lake or glacier, and voila – you've got yourself the best table in the house.

Remember, in Patagonia, every meal comes with a view. Whether it's jagged peaks, vast glaciers, or endless steppes, make sure to look up from your plate every now and then. After all, you're dining in one of the most beautiful places on Earth – soak it in, along with that extra glass of wine. Cheers to views that feed the soul as much as the food feeds the body!

Dining Etiquette and Local Foodie Tips

Eat Like a Local: Patagonian Food Hacks and Table Manners

Alright, foodie adventurers, let's talk about navigating Patagonia's culinary scene like a pro. Forget everything you know about dining etiquette – we're in gaucho country now!

First things first: timing. In Patagonia, lunch is a leisurely affair, often stretching from 1 PM to 3 PM. And dinner? Don't even think about showing up at a restaurant before 9 PM unless you want to dine with the tumbleweeds. Patagonians eat late, party later, and somehow still manage to scale mountains at dawn. It's a superpower, really.

Now, let's talk mate. This caffeine-packed herbal tea isn't just a drink; it's a social ritual. If someone offers you a mate, it's like they're extending the hand of friendship. The catch? Everyone shares the same metal straw (bombilla). Maintain composure, for this is an integral aspect of the journey. Just remember: don't say "gracias" until you're done, or they'll think you're refusing more. Rookie mistake.

When it comes to asado (barbecue), patience is key. This isn't your backyard grill-and-go. Asados can last for hours, with different cuts of meat appearing as if by magic throughout the afternoon. Pace yourself, amigo. And whatever you do, don't ask for ketchup. That's a one-way ticket to culinary exile.

Here's a hot tip: learn the art of 'el postre'. In Patagonia, dessert isn't just the sweet thing at the end of the meal. It's a whole other round of socializing. Even if you're stuffed, accept the offer. It's prime time for juicy gossip and hilarious stories.

Now, about tipping. In most Patagonian restaurants, a 10% tip is standard. But here's the twist: in some places, it's already included as a 'servicio' charge. Check your bill before double-tipping, unless you want to be known as the overly generous gringo (actually, that might not be so bad).

When dining in someone's home, bring a gift. Wine is always appreciated, but if you really want to impress, bring some mate gourd decorations or a fancy bombilla. You'll be the subject of everyone's conversation in a positive way.

Here's something that might throw you: in many Patagonian restaurants, you don't ask for the check. You just get up and head to the cashier when you're done. Patiently awaiting the bill while seated at an unoccupied table? That's a great way to accidentally spend the night.

If you're invited to a Patagonian home for dinner, don't show up on time. Seriously. Arriving 15-30 minutes late is the norm. Any earlier and you might catch your host still in their bathrobe. Fashionably late is always in fashion here.

When it comes to eating, Patagonians have a 'no waste' policy. If you're served a whole fish, expect to eat the cheeks and even the eyes. It's considered the best part. Don't make that face – it's actually delicious!

Here's a fun one: in Patagonia, burping after a meal isn't rude – it's a compliment to the chef. Okay, I'm kidding about this one. Please don't burp at the table. But wouldn't it be great if that were true?

Last but not least, learn to love Fernet and Coke. This bitter Italian liqueur mixed with cola is the unofficial drink of Patagonia. It's an acquired taste, but once you're hooked, you're hooked for life.

dining in Patagonia is about more than just food. It's about connection, storytelling, and experiencing life at a different pace. So pull up a chair, grab a fork (or a bombilla), and get ready to eat, drink, and live like a true Patagonian. Your taste buds and social gatherings will be delighted with your culinary creations.

CHAPTER 5: THINGS TO DO AND OUTDOOR ACTIVITIES

Patagonia is an outdoor enthusiast's paradise, offering a smorgasbord of adventures that cater to every level of thrill-seeker. From challenging hiking trails that wind through ancient forests and alongside towering glaciers, to serene kayaking expeditions in crystal-clear lakes and fjords, there's no shortage of ways to immerse yourself in the region's breathtaking natural beauty. For those seeking a bird's-eye view, hot air balloon rides provide an unforgettable perspective of the vast Patagonian landscape, while wildlife spotting excursions offer the chance to encounter the region's diverse fauna in their natural habitats.

The region's gardens and parks serve as perfect sanctuaries for those looking to explore at a more relaxed pace, showcasing the unique flora of Patagonia and offering tranquil spaces for reflection amidst the wild surroundings. Whether you're scaling a mountain, paddling through icy waters, or simply strolling through a botanical garden, each outdoor activity in Patagonia comes with its own set of unforgettable experiences and breathtaking vistas.

However, adventuring in Patagonia requires proper preparation and respect for the environment. The region's notoriously unpredictable weather, remote locations, and pristine ecosystems demand that visitors take necessary precautions and follow local guidelines. From packing appropriate gear to understanding leave-no-trace principles, being well-informed and prepared ensures not only a safe and enjoyable experience but also helps preserve Patagonia's natural wonders for future generations of adventurers.

Hiking Trails in the Patagonia

Lace up those boots and get ready for some of the most breathtaking hikes you'll ever experience! Patagonia's trails are calling, and trust me, you'll want to answer.

Let's start with the Laguna de los Tres trail in Argentina's Los Glaciares National Park. This 21km round trip is a real thigh-burner, but oh boy, is it worth it! As you reach the viewpoint, Mount Fitz Roy looms before you like a giant granite fortress. Pro tip: Start early and pack a thermos of hot mate tea - you'll thank me when you're sipping it with that million-dollar view.

For something a bit different, check out the Enchanted Forest Trail in Queulat National Park, Chile. This 3km path feels like stepping into a fairy tale. Mossy trees drip with lichens, and if you're lucky, you might spot a pudu (the world's smallest deer). The trail ends at a hanging glacier that looks like it's defying gravity. It's pure magic!

Fancy walking on ancient ice? The Big Ice trek on Perito Moreno Glacier is an absolute must. Strap on those crampons and explore a world of deep blue crevasses and ice caves. It's like being on another planet! Book with Hielo y Aventura in El Calafate (+54 2902 491138).

Now, if you're up for a real challenge, the Huemul Circuit in Argentina's Los Glaciares National Park is calling your name. This 4-day, 64km trek is not for the faint-hearted. You'll cross rivers on zip-lines, camp beside glaciers, and climb to viewpoints that'll make your jaw drop. There is no match for the unparalleled sense of fulfillment one experiences upon completion.

For a coastal adventure, hit the Wild Coast Trail in Cabo Froward, Chile. This 53km trail takes you to the southernmost point of continental South America. You'll walk along windswept beaches, through dense forests, and past shipwrecks. Keep an eye out for Magellanic penguins waddling along the shore!

Here's a hidden gem: the Cerro Castillo trek in Chile's Aysén region. Often overshadowed by Torres del Paine, this 4-day circuit offers turquoise lakes, jagged peaks, and way fewer crowds. The view of Cerro Castillo's castle-like spires reflecting in Laguna Cerro Castillo is pure postcard material.

Last but not least, don't miss the day hike to Laguna Esmeralda near Ushuaia. This 9km round trip takes you through peat bogs and lenga forests to a stunning emerald-green lagoon. On a calm day, the reflection of the surrounding mountains in the water is so perfect it'll make you question reality.

Remember, Patagonia's weather is as wild as its landscapes. Always check conditions before setting out, carry plenty of water, and leave no trace. Happy trails, fellow adventurers!

Kayaking and Canoeing Adventures

Ready to swap those hiking boots for a paddle? Patagonia's waterways are a playground for kayakers and canoeists, offering adventures that'll make your heart race and your soul sing.

Let's dive into the crystal-clear waters of Lago General Carrera in Chile. This stunning blue lake is home to the famous Marble Caves. Paddle through ethereal marble tunnels and caverns, marveling at how the water has sculpted the rock over millennia. The changing light creates a mesmerizing dance of colors on the cave walls. Book a tour with Patagonia Adventures in Puerto Río Tranquilo (+56 9 8889 5687) for an unforgettable experience.

For a wilder ride, head to the Futaleufú River in Chile. Known as the "Fu" by locals, this turquoise river is a whitewater enthusiast's dream. With rapids ranging from Class III to V+, it'll test your skills and pump your adrenaline. Even if you're not ready to tackle the big waves, watching the pros navigate the infamous "Terminator" rapid is a thrill in itself.

Fancy a multi-day paddling adventure? The Strait of Magellan won't disappoint. Launch from Punta Arenas and explore a maze of channels and fjords. Keep your eyes peeled for playful Peale's dolphins and majestic Andean condors soaring overhead. Just be prepared for those infamous Patagonian winds – they can turn a calm day into a challenging paddle in the blink of an eye.

For a more serene experience, glide through the otherworldly landscape of Laguna San Rafael National Park. Here, you can paddle right up to the face of the San Rafael Glacier. The sound of crackling ice and the occasional thunderous calving will send shivers down your spine. It's like being in nature's own IMAX theater!

Wildlife lovers, listen up! Kayaking in the Beagle Channel near Ushuaia is a must. Paddle alongside curious sea lions, watch Magellanic penguins porpoising through the water, and if you're lucky, you might even spot a minke whale. The backdrop of snow-capped mountains doesn't hurt either. Canal Fun (+54 2901 15551433) offers great guided tours.

Here's a hidden gem for you: Lago Puelo in Argentina. This lesser-known spot offers tranquil paddling with a stunning backdrop of Andean peaks. In the crystal-clear waters beneath your boat, fish gracefully glide and dart, creating an enchanting underwater ballet. Pack a picnic and spend the day exploring hidden beaches and coves.

Last but not least, for a true wilderness experience, brave the remote waters of Bernardo O'Higgins National Park in Chile. Paddle past towering glaciers, navigate through icebergs, and camp on pristine shores where few humans have set foot. Embarking on this journey is not for the faint of heart; however, the rewards are immeasurable.

Patagonia's waters can be as unpredictable as they are beautiful. Always check weather conditions, wear appropriate gear, and if you're not experienced, go with a guide. Now grab that paddle and get ready for some unforgettable aquatic adventures!

Hot Air Balloon Rides

Alright, adventurers, it's time to take your Patagonian experience to new heights – quite literally! Hot air ballooning over this wild landscape is like floating through a dream. Trust me, once you've seen Patagonia from the sky, you'll never look at it the same way again.

Let's start with a sunrise flight over the Andean foothills near San Carlos de Bariloche. As you drift silently above the mist-shrouded lakes and forests, the first rays of sunlight set the snow-capped peaks ablaze with color. It's pure magic! The folks at Globos Bariloche (+54 294 442-0566) will hook you up with an unforgettable ride.

For a truly unique experience, head to El Calafate for a balloon ride over the Patagonian steppe. As you float above the endless golden grasslands, you might spot herds of guanacos or even an elusive puma. And if you're lucky, you'll catch a glimpse of the massive Perito Moreno Glacier on the horizon. It's like being in your own private nature documentary!

Now, here's a hot tip: time your visit to coincide with the Villa La Angostura Balloon Festival in February. Dozens of colorful balloons fill the sky, creating a spectacle that'll have you grinning from ear to ear. You can even join in the fun with a tethered balloon ride if you're not quite ready for a full flight.

For those seeking a real adrenaline rush, why not try a hot air balloon ride over the Torres del Paine National Park in Chile? Soaring past those iconic granite spires is an experience that'll leave you breathless. Just imagine floating eye-level with condors as they ride the thermals! Book with Balloons Over Paine (+56 9 9231 5986) for this once-in-a-lifetime adventure.

Here's something you might not know: hot air ballooning in Patagonia isn't just a summer activity. In winter, you can take a magical flight over the snow-covered landscapes near Coyhaique. The contrast of white snow against dark forests is simply stunning. Plus, the crisp winter air allows for incredible visibility – on a clear day, you can see all the way to the Pacific Ocean!

For a truly off-the-beaten-path experience, check out the balloon flights over Tierra del Fuego. Floating above the "End of the World" is surreal – one minute you're over dense forests, the next you're gazing at the Beagle Channel stretching out to Antarctica. Keep your eyes peeled for shipwrecks along the coast – remnants of Patagonia's treacherous maritime history.

Last but not least, don't miss the chance to combine your balloon ride with a traditional Patagonian asado. Many operators offer post-flight celebrations where you can feast on succulent lamb while swapping stories of your aerial adventures. It's the perfect way to round off an unforgettable experience.

Remember, ballooning is weather-dependent, so be flexible with your plans. And don't forget to bring a camera – the views are out of this world! Now, who's ready to see Patagonia from a whole new perspective?

Wildlife Spotting Excursions

Get ready to channel your inner David Attenborough, folks! Patagonia's wildlife is as diverse and captivating as its landscapes. From furry giants to feathered acrobats, this corner of the world is a nature lover's paradise.

Let's kick things off with a visit to Punta Tombo in Argentina. This rocky peninsula is home to the largest colony of Magellanic penguins outside of Antarctica. Picture over a million of these tuxedo-clad cuties waddling around, squawking, and generally being adorable. Visit between September and April to see them in action. Pro tip: bring earplugs – these little guys can be noisy!

For a chance to spot the elusive puma, head to Torres del Paine National Park. These majestic big cats are notoriously shy, but with patience and a good guide, you might just get lucky. Tierra Patagonia Hotel (+56 2 2207 8861) offers fantastic puma tracking excursions. Just remember, it's their home – we're just visitors.

Now, how about something truly unique? The Valdés Peninsula is one of the few places in the world where you can witness orcas intentionally beaching themselves to catch sea lion pups. It's a heart-pounding spectacle of nature in action. February to April is prime time for this behavior. Keep your camera ready!

For bird lovers, the Los Glaciares National Park is a must-visit. Here, you can spot the mighty Andean condor soaring on thermal currents. Behold the majestic sight of these birds, with their awe-inspiring wingspans reaching up to 3.3 meters.Look out for their distinctive white "collar" as they glide overhead.

Fancy meeting some gentle giants? Take a boat trip in the Strait of Magellan to see humpback whales. These acrobatic cetaceans put on quite a show with their breaches and tail slaps. The folks at Solo Expediciones (+56 61 2229898) in Punta Arenas know all the best spots.

Here's a quirky one for you: head to Cabo Dos Bahías to see the Patagonian mara. These peculiar creatures look like a cross between a rabbit and a deer. They're monogamous and mate for life – how's that for relationship goals?

For a real treat, time your visit to Bahía Bustamante in Argentina between September and March. This remote coastal area becomes a breeding ground for the vulnerable Olrog's gull. It's one of only three known nesting sites for these rare birds.

Last but not least, don't miss the chance to spot the guanaco, Patagonia's very own camelid. These elegant creatures can be seen throughout the region, often in large herds. Watch out for the males – they have a habit of spitting when annoyed!

Remember, wildlife viewing requires patience and respect. Always follow your guide's instructions and never feed or approach the animals. Now go forth and explore – Patagonia's wild residents are waiting to amaze you!

Gardens and Parks to Explore

Alright, nature lovers, let's take a breather from the rugged wilderness and explore some of Patagonia's stunning gardens and parks. These green oases are perfect for when you need a moment of zen or just want to stretch your legs without scaling a mountain.

First up, let's wander through the enchanting Omora Ethnobotanical Park on Navarino Island, Chile. This place is a miniature wonderland! Grab a magnifying glass and explore the "Miniature Forests of Cape Horn" trail. You'll discover a hidden world of tiny lichens, mosses, and liverworts that'll blow your mind. It's like being in Honey, I Shrunk the Kids, but way cooler.

For a burst of color, head to the Jardín de la Patagonia in Punta Arenas. This botanical gem showcases over 50 species of regional flora. Keep an eye out for the vibrant Magellanic fuschia and the hardy calafate berry bush. Legend has it that if you eat a calafate berry, you're destined to return to Patagonia. Sounds like a tasty promise to me!

Now, how about a park with a side of history? Check out the Parque del Estrecho de Magallanes near Punta Arenas. It's not just about pretty plants here - you'll find replicas of indigenous Kawésqar huts and an exact copy of the Nao Victoria, Magellan's ship. Talk about a time-traveling garden experience!

For a quirky horticultural adventure, don't miss the Reserva Laguna Nimez in El Calafate. This urban nature reserve is home to flamingos, black-necked swans, and... wait for it... a cactus garden! Yep, cacti in Patagonia. It's like finding a penguin in the Sahara, but it works!

Here's a hidden gem for you: the Jardín de los Sentidos in Ushuaia. This sensory garden is designed to be enjoyed by sight, touch, and smell. Close your eyes and let your nose guide you through aromatic herbs and flowers. It's a feast for the senses at the end of the world!

Plant nerds, listen up! The Arboretum Patagónico in Esquel is your paradise. This living museum houses over 120 tree species from around the world. Watch out for the "Dinosaur tree" (Araucaria araucana) - it's been around since the Jurassic period! Talk about old school.

For a park with a view, climb up to the Mirador Cerro de la Cruz in Puerto Natales. This hilltop park offers panoramic vistas of the town, the Última Esperanza Sound, and the distant Andean peaks. Bring a picnic and watch the sun paint the sky at dusk. Instagram gold, I tell you!

Last but not least, for a truly unique experience, visit the Glacier Garden at Estancia Cristina. Accessible only by boat, this remote garden sits in the shadow of the Upsala Glacier. The juxtaposition of cultivated flowers against the wild glacial landscape is simply surreal.

Remember, folks, these parks and gardens are living treasures. Stick to the paths, don't pick the flowers, and take only memories (and maybe a few photos). Now go forth and find your own little slice of Patagonian paradise!

Outdoor Adventure Tips

Alright, adrenaline junkies and nature enthusiasts, listen up! Patagonia is an outdoor playground like no other, but it can also be as unpredictable as a cat on caffeine. Here's your crash course in staying safe while having the time of your life.

First things first: the weather. Patagonia's climate is like a moody teenager – it can change faster than you can say "where's my windbreaker?" Pack layers, folks. I'm talking thermal undies, fleece, waterproof jacket – the works. And always, ALWAYS carry a warm hat and gloves, even in summer. Trust me, your ears will thank you when that icy wind kicks up.

Now, let's talk about the infamous Patagonian wind. This isn't your average breeze – it's like Mother Nature's own personal hair dryer set to max. When hiking, keep your center of gravity low on windy ridges. And for the love of llamas, secure your tent properly! At 3 AM, pursuing a runaway tent is an undesirable activity.

Water is your best friend out here. Streams might look crystal clear, but they're often hosting a party for some nasty bacteria. Bring a good water filter or purification tablets. And speaking of water, if you're kayaking or rafting, respect the rivers. They're powerful and unforgiving – always wear a life jacket and helmet.

Let's chat about wildlife. Yes, Patagonia's critters are amazing, but remember – you're in their home. Keep your distance from pumas, guanacos, and even those cute penguins. And please, don't feed the animals. A fed animal is a dead animal, as the saying goes.

If you're heading into the backcountry, tell someone your plans. Better yet, register with the park rangers. It's like leaving a trail of breadcrumbs, but way more effective when you need help. And always carry a basic first aid kit – blisters and scrapes are like unwanted souvenirs out here.

Here's a tip many forget: protect your eyes! The sun reflecting off snow and water can be brutal. Bring good sunglasses and plenty of sunscreen. Getting sunburned in Patagonia is like getting sand in your swimsuit – uncomfortable and totally avoidable.

Now, let's talk navigation. GPS is great, but batteries die and signals fail. Always carry a good old-fashioned map and compass, and know how to use them. It's like having a superhero power when your phone goes kaput.

Lastly, embrace the Leave No Trace principles. Pack out what you pack in, stay on marked trails, and be mindful of fragile vegetation. Think of Patagonia as your grandmother's antique shop – look, admire, but don't break anything!

Remember, the goal is to have amazing adventures AND come back in one piece to brag about them. So gear up, stay alert, and get ready for the experience of a lifetime. Patagonia's waiting for you – just don't forget your common sense at home!

CHAPTER 6: ART, CULTURE AND ENTERTAINMENT

Patagonia isn't just about breathtaking landscapes and heart-pumping adventures – it's got a vibrant cultural scene that'll tickle your senses and warm your soul. From colorful local markets brimming with handcrafted treasures to museums showcasing the region's rich history, there's always something to discover. You might find yourself admiring intricate Mapuche textiles one moment and dancing the night away at a lively peña the next.

As you wander through charming towns, you'll stumble upon quaint galleries featuring works by local artists, their canvases capturing the wild beauty of Patagonia. Don't be surprised if you're suddenly swept up in a festive parade or find yourself tempted by the aroma of freshly baked chipa at a bustling street fair. The region's calendar is packed with events celebrating everything from Welsh tea traditions to gaucho culture.

When the sun sets, Patagonia comes alive in a different way. Cozy bars serve up locally brewed beers and cocktails infused with Calafate berries, while live music venues pulse with the rhythms of Andean folk and modern rock. And let's not forget the shopping – whether you're hunting for a warm alpaca sweater, a mate gourd, or a piece of unique jewelry, you'll find plenty of souvenirs to remind you of your Patagonian adventure long after you've returned home.

Local Arts and Crafts

Get ready to feast your eyes on some seriously cool handmade goodies, folks! Patagonia's local arts and crafts scene is like a colorful patchwork quilt of cultures and traditions. Trust me, you'll want to clear some space in your suitcase for these treasures.

Let's kick things off with the Mapuche textiles. These aren't your average blankets and ponchos – they're wearable works of art! Each piece tells a story through intricate geometric patterns and vibrant colors. Pop into the Lalen Kuze cooperative in Junín de los Andes to watch the weavers in action. The rhythmic clack of the looms is oddly soothing, I promise.

Now, hold onto your hats because we're diving into the world of gaucho crafts. These cowboys aren't just good with horses – they're master leather workers too. Check out the beautifully tooled belts, bags, and saddles at the Feria Artesanal in San Martín de los Andes. Pro tip: a mate gourd and bombilla (metal straw) make for a great souvenir. Just be prepared for some raised eyebrows at customs!

For something truly unique, head to Puerto Natales and hunt for crafts made from guanaco bone and horn. These materials have been used by indigenous people for centuries, and modern artisans are keeping the tradition alive with beautiful jewelry and decorative items. It's eco-friendly too – no guanacos are harmed in the making!

Ceramic lovers, you're in for a treat in Trelew. The Welsh settlers brought their pottery skills with them, and boy, have the locals run with it! Look out for delicate porcelain pieces decorated with native

Patagonian flowers. They're perfect for serving that Welsh tea you'll inevitably become addicted to.

Here's a quirky one for you: wood carving in Ushuaia. Thanks to the abundance of lenga trees, local artisans create everything from delicate bird figurines to intricate maze-like puzzles. Pop into the Paseo de los Artesanos to see the carvers at work. The scent of fresh wood shavings is bonus.

For a real hidden gem, seek out the felt artisans of the Chubut Valley. These folks take raw wool and transform it into the coziest slippers, hats, and even quirky animal figurines you've ever seen. It's like wearing a cloud on your feet!

Don't forget to check out the silver filigree work in Bariloche. This delicate jewelry-making technique was brought over by European immigrants, and local artisans have added their own Patagonian flair. A silver mate straw? Now that's traveling in style!

Lastly, keep an eye out for indigenous-inspired rock art reproductions. Local artists recreate ancient cave paintings on small canvases or even smooth river stones. It's like holding a piece of 10,000-year-old history in your hand.

Remember, buying local crafts isn't just about scoring cool souvenirs – it's about supporting traditional skills and local economies. So go ahead, treat yourself to that hand-knitted guanaco wool sweater. Your body will thank you when that Patagonian wind kicks up!

Museums and Galleries

Alright, culture vultures, let's dive into Patagonia's treasure trove of museums and galleries! These places aren't just stuffy rooms full of old stuff – they're like time machines mixed with art explosions. Trust me, even if you're not usually a museum person, these spots will knock your socks off.

First stop: the Museo Paleontológico Egidio Feruglio in Trelew. Buckle up, because we're going back in time – way back. We're talking dinosaurs, people! This place houses the bones of the largest known dinosaur, the Patagotitan mayorum. It's so big they had to build the museum around it! Pro tip: go for the nighttime tour. Dino skeletons look extra spooky in the dark.

Now, for something completely different, check out the Museo Nao Victoria in Punta Arenas. It's not every day you get to climb aboard exact replicas of famous ships, including Magellan's Victoria and Darwin's Beagle. Just try not to shout "Land ho!" Avoid speaking too loudly, as it may seem like you've lost control.

Art lovers, make a beeline for the Museo de Arte Eduardo Minnicelli in Río Gallegos. This funky converted water tower is packed with contemporary Patagonian art. The circular layout means you might get a bit dizzy, but in a good, art-induced way.

Here's a quirky one: the Museo del Mate in Campo de Herrera. Yep, a whole museum dedicated to yerba mate! Learn about the history of Argentina's favorite drink, check out mate gourds from different eras, and of course, sample some yourself. Caffeine buzz included free of charge!

History buffs, you can't miss the Museo Antropológico Martín Gusinde in Puerto Williams. It's the southernmost museum in the world! Dive into the fascinating culture of the Yaghan people, the original inhabitants of Tierra del Fuego. Warning: their traditional clothing (or lack thereof) might make you feel a bit chilly.

For a real hidden gem, seek out the Museo Leleque near Esquel. Owned by the Benetton family (yes, those Benettons), it tells the story of Patagonian settlers through a treasure trove of artifacts. From gaucho gear to Mapuche silver, it's like rummaging through Patagonia's ultimate attic.

Photography enthusiasts, the Centro de Fotografía Isla Negra in Puerto Natales is your paradise. This tiny gallery showcases stunning shots of Torres del Paine and beyond. It'll either inspire you to up your Instagram game or make you want to throw your camera into a glacier lake in despair.

Last but not least, the Museo Glaciarium near El Calafate is a must-visit. It's all about glaciers, baby! Interactive exhibits explain the science behind these icy giants, and there's even an ice bar where you can sip whiskey chilled by millennia-old glacier ice. Talk about a cool experience!

Remember, many of these museums offer guided tours in English, but booking ahead is smart. And don't be shy about chatting with the staff – they're usually bursting with fascinating tidbits that didn't make it onto the info plaques. Now go forth and get your culture on, Patagonia style!

Festivals and Events

Buckle up, party people! Patagonia's festival scene is as wild and varied as its landscapes. From quirky small-town fiestas to major cultural bashes, there's always something happening that'll make you want to throw your hands in the air and shout "¡Vamos!"

Let's kick things off with the Festival Nacional del Asado con Cuero in Cholila. Picture this: an entire festival dedicated to lamb barbecue. That's right, for three glorious days in February, the air is filled with the mouthwatering aroma of slow-roasted lamb. Vegetarians, you might want to bring a nose clip!

For a totally different vibe, hit up the Fiesta Nacional del Trekking in El Chaltén every March. It's like a hiker's paradise come to life, with guided treks, gear expos, and even a mountain film festival. The highlight? A massive asado (because of course) where you can swap trail stories with fellow trekking enthusiasts.

Now, here's one for the history books: the Aniversario del Primer Izamiento de la Bandera Argentina en las Islas Malvinas. Try saying that five times fast! This solemn ceremony in Ushuaia on November 6th commemorates the first raising of the Argentine flag in the Falkland Islands. This serves as a poignant reflection on the intricate historical tapestry of the region.

Music lovers, don't miss the Festivales Musicales de Bariloche. This week-long classical music extravaganza in February turns the entire town into a concert hall. Imagine listening to Beethoven with the Andes as your backdrop. Classy, right?

For something truly unique, check out the Fiesta del Curanto in Colonia Suiza near Bariloche. This annual event in February celebrates the traditional Mapuche-German fusion dish, curanto. Watch as locals unearth steaming pots from underground ovens, then dig into this hearty meat-and-veggie feast. It's like a culinary treasure hunt!

Adrenaline junkies, the Festival de la Aventura in San Martín de los Andes is calling your name. Held in November, it's a week-long celebration of all things outdoorsy. From mountain biking competitions to paragliding demos, it's like an extreme sports buffet. Just remember: watching the pros doesn't make you one!

Here's a quirky one: the Fiesta Nacional de la Esquila in Río Mayo. This "National Shearing Festival" in January is exactly what it sounds like. Watch skilled shearers compete to de-fleece sheep at lightning speed. It's oddly mesmerizing, and you'll gain a whole new appreciation for your wool sweater.

For a splash of color, don't miss the Carnaval de Invierno in Ushuaia. This winter carnival in July turns the "End of the World" into a Rio-style party, complete with elaborate costumes and street parades. Who says you can't samba in snow boots?

Last but not least, the Fiesta Nacional del Salmón in Camarones is a fish lover's dream. Held in February, it celebrates the return of salmon to Patagonian waters. Expect cooking contests, fishing tournaments, and enough seafood to make you sprout gills.

Remember, folks, festival dates can shift, so always double-check before planning your trip. And don't forget to pack your dancing shoes –

you never know when you might find yourself doing the chacarera under the southern stars!

Nightlife and Entertainment

Think Patagonia's all about early nights and glacier treks? Think again! When the sun goes down, this wild region knows how to party. Let's dive into the after-dark scene that'll have you howling at the moon (or maybe just at your mate's dance moves).

First stop: Ushuaia, the world's southernmost city. Hit up Dublin Bar for a pint at the "end of the world." It's got live music, great beer, and enough Irish charm to make you forget you're in Argentina. Just don't challenge the locals to a Guinness-drinking contest – they've had practice!

For a true Patagonian night out, you can't miss a peña. These folk music gatherings are like stepping into a living, breathing, guitar-strumming history book. Check out La Peña del Indio in El Calafate. Don't worry if you can't tell your chacarera from your zamba – just clap along and pretend you know what you're doing.

Now, if you're feeling lucky, Bariloche's got you covered. Casino de Bariloche isn't Vegas, but it's got enough roulette wheels and slot machines to keep things interesting. Pro tip: set a budget before you go in. Those Patagonian views don't pay for themselves!

For something totally unique, head to Cerro Otto in Bariloche. This rotating mountaintop restaurant does a full 360° every 20 minutes. Sip cocktails as the landscape spins by – it's like being in a slow-motion disco ball with a view. Just don't spin too fast on your way to the bathroom!

Craft beer fans, listen up! Punta Arenas is becoming a hoppy heaven. Austral Brewery offers night tours where you can sample their famous Calafate beer. Legend has it that eating (or drinking) Calafate berries means you'll return to Patagonia. Bottoms up!

If you're in Puerto Madryn, don't miss Cheester. This quirky bar is decked out like an old ship, complete with portholes and nautical knick-knacks. Order a "Tsunami" cocktail and watch the bartenders put on a show. Just don't blame us if you're a bit "seasick" the next morning.

For a dash of sophistication, check out the Gran Hotel Termas de Chillán in Chile. Their piano bar is the perfect spot for a nightcap after a day of skiing or soaking in the hot springs. Sip a pisco sour and pretend you're in a James Bond movie.

Now, if you want to dance till dawn, head to El Bodegón in El Calafate. This place starts as a cozy restaurant and transforms into a pulsing nightclub. By 2 AM, you'll be doing the tango with your new best friends. Don't worry, everyone looks good dancing after a few Fernet and Colas!

For a truly memorable night, time your visit with the full moon and join a nocturnal trek in Torres del Paine. Watching the moonlight glint off the glaciers is like being on another planet. Just don't get so mesmerized you wander off a cliff!

Remember, Patagonian nights can be chilly, so layer up before you head out. And pace yourself – the altitude can make those cocktails hit harder than you expect. Now go on, paint the town red... or maybe glacier blue!

Local Markets, Shopping, and Souvenirs

Alright, shopaholics and souvenir hunters, get ready to flex those bargaining muscles! Patagonia's markets and shops are treasure troves of unique goodies that'll make your friends back home green with envy.

Let's start with the Feria Artesanal in Ushuaia. This open-air market is a riot of colors and smells. You'll find everything from hand-knitted guanaco wool sweaters to quirky penguin-shaped mate gourds. Pro tip: bring cash and an extra bag – you'll need both!

For a taste of Welsh Patagonia, head to Trelew's Mercado Artesanal. It's like stepping into a time warp where tea cozies meet gaucho knives. Don't miss the alfajores – these dulce de leche-filled cookies are addictive. Buy extra, trust me.

Now, if you're in El Calafate, make a beeline for Paseo de los Artesanos. It's a long street lined with craft stalls and shops. Keep an eye out for jewelry made from Patagonian stones – each piece is like wearing a little bit of the Andes.

Here's a quirky one: the Mercado Municipal in Punta Arenas. Sure, you can buy fresh produce, but the real treasures are in the odds and ends section. Vintage Magellanic maps, anyone? Or how about a keychain made from a sheep's hoof? It's weird, it's wonderful, it's pure Patagonia.

Chocolate lovers, listen up! Bariloche is your paradise. Calle Mitre is lined with chocolate shops that'll make Willy Wonka jealous. Try the chocolate-covered calafate berries at Mamuschka – they're like blueberries with superpowers.

For serious shoppers, Puerto Natales' Zona Franca is a duty-free shopper's dream. Stock up on outdoor gear, electronics, and yes, more chocolate. Just remember, there are limits on how much you can take out of Chile.

Here's a hidden gem: the Mercado de Pulgas in Comodoro Rivadavia. This flea market is where locals buy and sell everything under the sun. You might find vintage Patagonian postcards, old gaucho tools, or that lava lamp you never knew you needed.

Don't leave Patagonia without visiting a real gaucho store. Talabartería El Bagual in San Martín de los Andes is the real deal. As soon as you step inside, the pungent aroma of leather envelops your senses. From intricately tooled belts to full-on gaucho outfits, it's cowboy heaven.

For a modern twist on traditional crafts, check out Elemento Patagonia in Puerto Madryn. They've taken Mapuche designs and applied them to everything from laptop cases to surfboards. It's like traditional meets tech-savvy.

Last but not least, if you're in Coyhaique, don't miss the Feria Rural Ñirehuao. This monthly market is where local farmers and artisans gather to sell their wares. The honey here is liquid gold, and the homemade cheeses are to die for.

Remember, haggling is often expected in markets, but do it with a smile. And always ask before taking photos of artisans or their work. Now go forth and shop till you drop – just make sure you can still lift your suitcase at the end of it all!

CHAPTER 7: 7-DAY ITINERARY IN PATAGONIA

Day 1: Touchdown in Patagonia's Gateway - El Calafate

Morning:
As your plane descends into El Calafate International Airport, your heart races with anticipation. The vast Patagonian steppe stretches out below you, a sea of golden grass punctuated by glittering lakes. After touchdown, breathe in that crisp mountain air - you've arrived in adventure's paradise! Grab your bags and hop into a pre-arranged transfer (book with Cal-Tur at www.caltur.com.ar or +54 2902 491-196) for the short 20-minute ride into town.

Afternoon:
Check into your home for the next two nights, the charming Kosten Aike Hotel (Address: 407 Gobernador Moyano, El Calafate; Phone: +54 2902 492-424; www.kostenaike.com.ar). This cozy lodge, decorated with local Tehuelche art, is the perfect base for your Patagonian adventures. Once you've freshened up, stroll down Avenida del Libertador, El Calafate's main drag. Pop into Paseo de Los Artesanos (Address: 963 Av. del Libertador) to pick up some mate gourd souvenirs or handcrafted wool items.

Evening:
As the sun begins to set, painting the sky in breathtaking hues of pink and orange, make your way to La Tablita (Address: 1006 Coronel Rosales; Phone: +54 2902 491-065). This local institution has been

serving up succulent Patagonian lamb for over 50 years. Order the cordero a la estaca - lamb slow-roasted on a cross stake - and pair it with a robust Malbec from nearby Río Negro. As you savor each bite, chat with your waiter about tomorrow's glacier adventure. With a belly full of lamb and a head full of dreams about blue ice, amble back to your hotel. Tomorrow, the real Patagonian magic begins!

Day 2: Marveling at the Mighty Perito Moreno Glacier

Morning:
Rise and shine early for your big glacier day! Fuel up with a hearty breakfast at the hotel before your 8:00 AM pickup by Hielo y Aventura (www.hieloyaventura.com; +54 2902 491-998). The hour-long drive to Los Glaciares National Park flies by as your guide regales you with facts about the region's unique geography.

Afternoon:
Prepare for your jaw to drop as you first lay eyes on Perito Moreno Glacier. This massive wall of ice, stretching 5 km wide and towering 74 meters above Lago Argentino, is a breathtaking sight. Spend the next few hours exploring the walkways, listening to the thunderous cracks of calving ice, and marveling at the glacier's brilliant blue hues. For the adventurous, gear up for the Big Ice Trek (book in advance), where you'll don crampons and trek across the glacier's surface, peering into deep crevasses and sipping whiskey chilled with millennia-old glacial ice.

Evening:
Return to El Calafate with your senses overloaded and your camera full. For dinner, head to Pura Vida (Address: 907 Av. del Libertador; Phone:

+54 2902 496-475). This cozy restaurant offers a modern take on Patagonian cuisine. Try the trout ceviche or the guanaco carpaccio for a true taste of the region. As you relax with a glass of local wine, reflect on the day's icy adventures and get excited for tomorrow's journey to El Chaltén.

Day 3: Trekking Paradise - El Chaltén

Morning:
After breakfast, check out and board your bus to El Chaltén. The 3-hour journey through the Patagonian steppe is a visual feast, with guanacos grazing and condors soaring overhead. As you approach El Chaltén, the iconic spires of Mount Fitz Roy come into view, causing a collective gasp on the bus.

Afternoon:
Arrive in El Chaltén, Argentina's self-proclaimed 'Trekking Capital'. Check into the charming Don Los Cerros Boutique Hotel & Spa (Address: San Martín 260; Phone: +54 2962 493-182; www.donloscerros.com). After settling in, head to the visitor's center to pick up trail maps and get the latest weather forecast. Then, stretch your legs on the short but scenic Mirador Los Cóndores trail. This 2-hour round trip hike offers stunning views of the town, the Fitz Roy massif, and Cerro Torre.

Evening:
As the alpenglow paints Fitz Roy in shades of pink and gold, make your way to La Tapera (Address: Lionel Terray 780; Phone: +54 2962 493-139). This rustic restaurant is a favorite among climbers and hikers. Warm up with a hearty locro stew and toast to your upcoming trek with

a craft beer from the local El Chaltén Brewing Company. Turn in early tomorrow's a big hiking day!

Day 4: Conquering Laguna de los Tres

Morning:
It's alpine start time! Rise before dawn and grab a quick breakfast at the hotel. Hit the trail by 6:00 AM for the challenging but rewarding hike to Laguna de los Tres. The 20 km round trip takes about 8-9 hours, so pack plenty of water, snacks, and layers.

Afternoon:
After a grueling final ascent, you reach Laguna de los Tres. The view of Mount Fitz Roy reflected in the turquoise glacial lake is worth every drop of sweat. Find a comfortable rock, break out your packed lunch, and soak in the majestic Patagonian landscape. Take your time descending, stopping at miradors along the way for different perspectives of the mountains.

Evening:
Weary but elated, treat yourself to a well-deserved feast at Estepa (Address: San Martín 390; Phone: +54 2962 493-213). Their lamb ragout with homemade papardelle is the perfect reward for tired muscles. If you still have energy, swap trail stories with fellow hikers over a nightcap at La Cervecería (Address: San Martín 564).

Day 5: Journey to the End of the World - Ushuaia

Morning:
Bid farewell to El Chaltén and catch an early flight to Ushuaia via El Calafate. As you fly south, watch the landscape transform from

mountains to sea. Landing in Ushuaia, the world's southernmost city, you'll feel the thrill of being at the edge of the world.

Afternoon:
Check into the luxurious Arakur Ushuaia Resort & Spa (Address: Cerro Alarkén 1; Phone: +54 2901 444-000; www.arakur.com). Take the hotel's complimentary shuttle into town and visit the End of the World Museum (Address: Avenida Maipú 173; www.museomaritimo.com) to learn about the region's fascinating history and indigenous cultures.

Evening:
For dinner, head to Kaupé (Address: Roca 470; Phone: +54 2901 422-704). Perched on a hill overlooking the Beagle Channel, it offers spectacular views and equally impressive cuisine. Try the king crab or the locally caught sea bass. As you dine, raise a glass to Darwin, Magellan, and all the explorers who ventured to this remote corner of the world.

Day 6: Exploring the Beagle Channel

Morning:
After breakfast, make your way to the tourist port for a catamaran cruise of the Beagle Channel with Catamarán Canoero (Address: Maipú 1210; Phone: +54 2901 437-000; www.catamarancanoero.com). Keep your eyes peeled for playful sea lions, Magellanic penguins, and if you're lucky, breaching whales.

Afternoon:
Back on land, take a taxi to Tierra del Fuego National Park. Hike the coastal path to Lapataia Bay, where the Pan-American Highway

officially ends. Stand at the sign marking the 'End of the World' and contemplate the vast wilderness stretching south to Antarctica.

Evening:

For your final Patagonian dinner, visit Chez Manu (Address: Luis Pedro Fique 3560; Phone: +54 2901 432-253). French-born chef Emmanuel Herbin crafts exquisite dishes showcasing local ingredients like Fuegian spider crab and black hake. As you savor each bite, reflect on your Patagonian adventure and start planning your return trip!

Day 7: Farewell to Patagonia

Morning:

Enjoy a leisurely breakfast at Arakur, soaking in the panoramic views of the Beagle Channel one last time. If time allows, take a final stroll along Ushuaia's waterfront, breathing in the crisp sea air and pondering the adventures that await across those southern seas.

Afternoon:

Check out of your hotel and head to Ushuaia International Airport. As your plane takes off, gaze out at the snow-capped peaks and sparkling waters below. You're leaving with a camera full of photos, a heart full of memories, and an irresistible urge to return to this wild and beautiful edge of the world.

Evening:

As you wing your way home, close your eyes and replay the highlights of your Patagonian adventure – the thunderous calving of Perito Moreno, the jagged spires of Fitz Roy, the windswept beauty of Tierra del Fuego. You've experienced the raw power and pristine beauty of one of the world's last great wildernesses. Patagonia has left its mark on you, just as explorers and adventurers have been captivated by its untamed spirit for centuries.

CHAPTER 8: PRACTICAL INFORMATION AND TIPS

Etiquette and Customs in Patagonia: Dancing with the Wind

When you step into Patagonia, you're not just entering a new land you're stepping into a world where the wind shapes more than just the landscape. It molds the customs, the etiquette, and the very spirit of the people. So, let's waltz through some Patagonian dos and don'ts, shall we?

The Art of Mate Sipping:
Ah, mate – the lifeblood of Patagonia! This caffeine-packed herbal tea isn't just a drink; it's a social ritual. If someone offers you a mate, don't say no – it's like turning down a hug from your grandmother. But here's the tricky part: sip, don't slurp, and for the love of guanacos, don't say "gracias" until you're done. Why? Because "gracias" means you're tapping out of the sharing circle. Keep sipping until you're caffeinated to the eyeballs!

Timing is Everything:
Patagonians march to the beat of their own drum – or rather, to the rhythm of the wind. Dinner? Don't even think about it before 9 PM. Showing up "on time" to a party? You might end up helping set the table. Arrive fashionably late, around 10 PM, and you'll fit right in.

The Cheek-Kiss Tango:
Get ready to pucker up! Greeting friends (and sometimes strangers) with a kiss on the cheek is as Patagonian as glaciers and gauchos. But don't go in for the full smooch – it's more of an air kiss with a gentle cheek touch. Oh, and it's always right cheek to right cheek. Get it wrong, and you might end up in an awkward nose bump tango.

Sheep's Clothing:
In Patagonia, wearing wool isn't just fashion – it's practically a religion. But be careful about your choice of sweater. Wearing a cheaply made, mass-produced "alpaca" sweater from a tourist shop is like wearing a "I Love NY" t-shirt to a Yankees game. Opt for locally made, high-quality wool items instead. Your body will thank you when the infamous Patagonian wind kicks up!

The Asado Code:
If you're invited to an asado (barbecue), bring something to share wine is always a safe bet. But don't you dare touch that grill! The asador (grill master) is the undisputed king of the coals. Offering to help might be seen as questioning their grilling prowess. Instead, stand back, sip your wine, and marvel at the meat magic happening before you.

Nature's Call:
Patagonians have a deep respect for their wild, untamed land. If you're out hiking, remember the "leave no trace" principle. This includes your "business" – pack it out if you can't bury it properly. And whatever you do, don't pick the flowers. That delicate bloom you're eyeing might be a rare species that took centuries to grow in this harsh climate.

The Gear Faux Pas:

Yes, you're in Patagonia, home of the famous outdoor brand. But wearing head-to-toe Patagonia gear screams "tourist" louder than a startled guanaco. Mix it up with local brands or other outdoor wear. Patagonians appreciate good gear, but they appreciate subtlety even more.

Tipping the Scales:
Unlike in some parts of South America, tipping is expected in Patagonian restaurants and for services. But don't go overboard – 10% is usually sufficient. Over-tipping can make locals uncomfortable. Remember, in Patagonia, it's all about balance – like walking against the wind without being blown over.

The Photo Finesse:
Patagonia is a photographer's dream, but remember: not everything is a photo op. Always ask before snapping pictures of people, especially in indigenous communities. And for goodness' sake, don't use a selfie stick at a glacier viewpoint – you might end up photobombing someone else's once-in-a-lifetime shot.

The Silence of the Pampa:
Patagonians appreciate the sound of silence. If you're out in nature, keep the chatter and music to a minimum. Let the wind, the birds, and the creaking of glaciers be your playlist. After all, you've come all this way to experience Patagonia, not to hear your favorite pop songs echo across the steppe.

Remember, in Patagonia, the biggest faux pas is not embracing the spirit of the place. Be open, be respectful, and be ready to dance with the wind. Who knows? You might just find yourself feeling a little Patagonian by the end of your trip!

Language and Communication

Tongues of the Tierra: Language and Communication in Patagonia

Welcome to Patagonia, where the languages are as diverse as the landscapes! Buckle up, language lovers – we're about to embark on a linguistic journey that's as wild as a ride across the pampas.

Spanish with a Twist:
First things first – yes, Spanish is the main language here. But Patagonian Spanish? It's got more flavor than a juicy asado. You'll hear "che" peppered throughout conversations – it's like saying "hey" or "dude." And don't be surprised if you hear "vos" instead of "tú" for "you." It's not a mistake; it's just how they roll down here.

The Whisper of Welsh:
Believe it or not, there's a pocket of Patagonia where you might hear "bore da" (good morning) instead of "buenos días." The Welsh colony in Chubut Province has been keeping their language alive since 1865. Pop into a tearoom in Gaiman, and you might just find yourself in a linguistic time warp!

Indigenous Voices:
Listen closely, and you might catch whispers of Mapudungun, the language of the Mapuche people. Words like "Nahuel" (tiger) and "Huapi" (island) have snuck into place names all over Patagonia. It's like a linguistic treasure hunt – see how many you can spot!

The Gaucho's Grunt:
Gauchos, those legendary Patagonian cowboys, have their own way of talking. It's not just Spanish; it's Spanish with a healthy dose of horse sense. Learn terms like "pirca" (stone wall) and "tranquera" (gate), and you'll be speaking gaucho in no time.

Sign Language of the South:
In the vast expanses of Patagonia, sometimes a gesture speaks louder than words. A chin lift means "over there," while a pout with raised eyebrows means "I don't know." Master these, and you'll be communicating like a local even when the legendary Patagonian wind drowns out your words.

The Eloquence of Silence:
Patagonians appreciate the art of comfortable silence. Don't feel the need to fill every moment with chatter. Sometimes, a shared mate and a view of the Andes say more than words ever could.

English: The Glacier Bridge:
With tourism booming, English is becoming the lingua franca in many tourist hotspots. Don't anticipate widespread fluency in the language. Your efforts to speak Spanish will be appreciated, even if you sound like you're gargling gravel.

The Dialect of Distance:
In a land this vast, regional dialects can vary wildly. What's "cool" in Ushuaia might be "groovy" in El Calafate. Embrace the diversity – it's like getting multiple trips in one!

Nature's Vocabulary:

Patagonia has its own natural language. Learn to read the clouds for incoming weather, understand the call of the caracara bird, and interpret the cracks of a glacier. It's a vocabulary that goes beyond words.

The Tone of Time:

Time moves differently here. "Ahora" (now) might mean in five minutes, or in an hour. It's not rudeness; it's just Patagonian time. Learn to go with the flow, and you'll find yourself speaking the language of laid-back living in no time.

Nonverbal Nuggets:

Personal space? In Patagonia, it's more of a suggestion than a rule. Don't be surprised if conversations happen at close quarters. It's not intrusive; it's intimate.

The Rhythm of the Region:

Patagonian Spanish has a unique cadence, influenced by the land itself. It rises and falls like the Andean peaks, and flows smoothly like glacial rivers. Tune your ear to this rhythm, and you'll be dancing the linguistic tango in no time.

Remember, in Patagonia, communication goes beyond words. It's in the shared sip of mate, the nod of understanding as you both gaze at Fitz Roy, the collective gasp as a chunk of Perito Moreno calves into the lake. So open your ears, your eyes, and your heart. In this land of extremes, every interaction is a chance to learn a new language – the language of Patagonia itself.

Simple Language Phrases

Patagonian Phrase Power: Your Lingo Lifeline

Greetings & Goodbyes:
1. "Buen día, che" (bwen DEE-ah cheh) - Good day, mate
2. "Chau, nos vemos" (chow, nohs VEH-mohs) - Bye, see you later

Weather Talk (because it's always a topic):
3. "Hace un frío bárbaro" (AH-seh un FREE-oh BAR-ba-roh) - It's freezing cold
4. "El viento está bravo hoy" (el vee-EN-toh es-TAH BRA-voh oy) - The wind is fierce today

Outdoor Adventures:
5. "¿Dónde empieza el sendero?" (DOHN-deh em-pee-EH-sah el sen-DEH-roh) - Where does the trail start?
6. "Necesito un mapa" (neh-seh-SEE-toh un MA-pa) - I need a map

Food & Drink:
7. "Un mate, por favor" (un MA-teh, por fa-VOR) - A mate, please
8. "Está riquísimo" (es-TAH ree-KEE-see-moh) - This is delicious

Wildlife Spotting:
9. "¡Mira, un guanaco!" (MEE-rah, un gwa-NA-koh) - Look, a guanaco!
10. "¿Dónde se pueden ver pingüinos?" (DOHN-deh seh PWEH-den ver pin-GWEEN-ohs) - Where can we see penguins?

Emergency Phrases:

11. "Necesito ayuda" (neh-seh-SEE-toh ah-YOO-dah) - I need help
12. "¿Dónde está el hospital?" (DOHN-deh es-TAH el os-pee-TAL) - Where's the hospital?

Shopping & Services:
13. "¿Cuánto cuesta?" (KWAN-toh KWES-tah) - How much does it cost?
14. "¿Aceptan tarjetas?" (ah-SEP-tan tar-HEH-tas) - Do you accept cards?

Transportation:
15. "¿A qué hora sale el bus?" (ah keh O-rah SA-leh el boos) - What time does the bus leave?
16. "Necesito un taxi" (neh-seh-SEE-toh un TAK-see) - I need a taxi

Accommodation:
17. "¿Tienen habitaciones libres?" (tee-EH-nen ah-bee-tah-see-OH-nes LEE-bres) - Do you have any free rooms?
18. "¿Hay wifi?" (eye wee-fee) - Is there wifi?

Local Slang:
19. "Estoy re cansado" (es-TOY reh kan-SA-doh) - I'm super tired
20. "Qué copado" (keh ko-PA-doh) - How cool

Cultural Appreciation:
21. "La Patagonia es hermosa" (la pa-ta-GO-nyah es er-MO-sah) - Patagonia is beautiful
22. "Me encanta la cultura de acá" (meh en-KAN-ta la kul-TU-ra deh ah-KAH) - I love the culture here

Remember, Patagonian Spanish has a unique melody. It's like the wind whistling through the Andes - sometimes soft, sometimes strong, but always with a distinctive rhythm. Don't worry about perfect pronunciation; locals will appreciate your effort to speak their language.

Pro tip: Learn to elongate your vowels slightly, especially at the end of sentences. It's a subtle way to sound more local. For example, "Gracias" becomes "Graciaaas" (gra-SEE-ahs).

Lastly, remember that language in Patagonia is as much about what you don't say as what you do. A knowing nod while sipping mate can speak volumes. A gesture towards the mountains might replace a whole sentence. And sometimes, a simple "che" with the right intonation can express a whole range of emotions.

So go forth, language adventurer! With these phrases in your arsenal, you're ready to chat with gauchos, banter with shopkeepers, and maybe even whisper sweet nothings to a curious guanaco. Just remember - in Patagonia, the best conversations often happen over a shared mate, under a star-studded sky, with the wind carrying your words across the vast, beautiful wilderness.

Health and Safety Tips

Stay Safe and Sound in the Land of Giants

Welcome to Patagonia, where the landscapes are as breathtaking as they are unforgiving. Here's how to keep your adventure epic, not tragic:

Tame the Wind:
Patagonian wind isn't just strong; it's like nature's own WWE wrestler. It can knock you off balance faster than you can say "guanaco." Always face the wind when opening car doors to avoid them becoming instant sails. And ladies, those flowy dresses? Save them for the tango halls in Buenos Aires.

Sun Smarts:
The Patagonian sun is sneaky. It might feel cool, but the UV rays are having a party on your skin. Slather on that sunscreen like it's your job. And those stylish sunglasses? They're not just for looks – the glare off glaciers can be blinding.

Hydration Station:
Patagonia's dry air will suck the moisture right out of you. Carry water everywhere, even if you think you don't need it. Your future self will thank you when you're not hallucinating that a guanaco is your long-lost cousin.

Altitude Attitude:
Heading to the Andes? Take it slow, amigo. Altitude sickness is no joke. It's like the world's worst hangover, minus the fun night before. Ascend gradually, stay hydrated, and maybe skip that second glass of Malbec for the first few days.

Glacier Smarts:
Glaciers are cool (pun intended), but they're not playgrounds. Keep a respectful distance. That blue ice might look solid, but it could be hiding crevasses deeper than your existential crisis.

Wildlife Wisdom:
Patagonian wildlife is amazing, but remember – you're in their home. Don't try to pet the pumas or take selfies with sea lions. And if a guanaco spits at you, take it as a compliment – you've been officially welcomed to Patagonia!

Trail Mix Tricks:
Hiking the iconic trails? Pack snacks like you're preparing for hibernation. Trail mix, dried fruit, and chocolate are your new best friends. Nothing ruins a view faster than a grumbling stomach.

Weather Whims:
Patagonian weather is like a moody teenager – it changes rapidly and without warning. Layer up, even if it looks sunny. That t-shirt and shorts combo might leave you chattering like a Magellanic penguin.

Buddy System:
Going off the beaten path? Buddy up! Solo adventures sound romantic, but having someone to share the view (and potentially call for help) is priceless. Plus, you'll need someone to pinch you to make sure you're not dreaming.

Insect Intelligence:
In summer, Patagonian bugs come out to play. Pack insect repellent, or risk becoming an all-you-can-eat buffet for mosquitoes. And those cute little black flies? They bite. Hard.

Road Trip Readiness:
Driving the vast Patagonian roads? Fill up whenever you can. Gas stations can be as rare as a calm day in Tierra del Fuego. And always carry extra water and snacks – road trip munchies are universal.

Campfire Caution:
If you're camping, keep those fires small and controlled. Patagonian wind can turn a cozy campfire into a wildfire faster than you can say "asado."

Packing for Extremes:
When packing for a summer trip, include clothes for different weather conditions. Patagonia laughs in the face of weather forecasts. That sunny day can turn into a mini ice age in minutes.

Elevation Elation:
Hiking at higher elevations? Take breaks, even if you feel fine. It's not lazy; it's smart. Use these breaks to soak in the view and remind yourself that yes, this is real life.

Local Knowledge is Gold:
Chat with locals about conditions before heading out. They know the land better than any app or guidebook. Plus, it's a great excuse to practice your Spanish!

Emergency Prep:
Know the local emergency numbers. In Argentina, it's 911 for police and 107 for ambulances. In Chile, it's 133 for police and 131 for ambulances. Save them in your phone – hoping you'll never need them, but being glad you have them.

The goal is to return home with epic stories, not epic hospital bills. Stay alert, respect nature, and embrace the Patagonian spirit of adventure – just with a healthy dose of common sense. Now go forth and conquer those landscapes, you intrepid explorer!

Emergency Contacts

Patagonian Lifelines: Your Emergency Contact Cheat Sheet

When the Unexpected Strikes in the Land of Extremes

Let's face it, even in a place as magical as Patagonia, sometimes things go sideways. Maybe you've had a tango with a thorny calafate bush, or your attempt to speak guanaco didn't go as planned. Whatever the crisis, big or small, we've got you covered. Here's your go-to guide for emergency contacts in Patagonia. Keep this handy – it might just be your ticket out of a pickle!

Argentina's Golden Numbers:
- General Emergency: 911 (Yes, just like in the movies!)
- Police: 101 (For when you need to report a rogue penguin)
- Fire Department: 100 (In case your asado skills need professional backup)
- Medical Emergency: 107 (When that "small blister" turns into a monster)

Chile's Hotlines:
- General Emergency: 131 (One number to rule them all)
- Police: 133 (Carabineros, at your service)
- Fire Department: 132 (Bomberos, ready to douse your troubles)
- Search and Rescue: 137 (ONEMI - for when you're really, really lost)

Mountain Rescue Heroes:
- Argentina: +54 294 4422772 (Club Andino Bariloche)
- Chile: +56 2 2639 8175 (Socorro Andino)

Embassies - Your Home Away From Home:
- U.S. Embassy in Argentina: +54 11 5777 4533
- U.S. Embassy in Chile: +56 2 2330 3000
- UK Embassy in Argentina: +54 11 4808 2200
- UK Embassy in Chile: +56 2 2370 4100
- Australian Embassy in Argentina: +54 11 4779 3500
- Australian Embassy in Chile: +56 2 2550 3500

For other nationalities, check your embassy's website before you go. They're like your country's living room in a foreign land!

Local Lifesavers:
- El Calafate Hospital: +54 2902 491-297
- Ushuaia Hospital: +54 2901 423-200
- Punta Arenas Hospital: +56 61 2293000

National Parks - When Nature Calls (For Help):
- Los Glaciares National Park (Argentina): +54 2962 493-045
- Torres del Paine National Park (Chile): +56 61 2360425

Lost in Translation? Language Helplines:
- Argentina: 0800-999-3368 (Free language assistance)
- Chile: 800 835 133 (Dial 1 for English support)

Weather Warnings:
- Argentina: www.smn.gob.ar
- Chile: www.meteochile.gob.cl

Because in Patagonia, the weather can change faster than a chameleon at a disco!

Tech Troubles:
- Argentina: 112 (For mobile phone emergencies)
- Chile: 103 (When your lifeline to Instagram fails)

Road Assistance:
- Argentina: 0800-333-1680 (ACA - Automóvil Club Argentino)
- Chile: 600 600 2000 (AutoClub Chile)

For when your road trip turns into an unexpected camping adventure.

Poison Control:
- Argentina: 0800-333-0160
- Chile: +56 2 2635 3800

In case that "edible" berry wasn't so edible after all.

Animal Encounters Gone Wild:
- Argentina Wildlife Rescue: +54 11 4781-8010
- Chile Wildlife Service: +56 2 2345 7100

For when you need to report a guanaco gang or a penguin parade gone rogue. Your best emergency contact is often the person standing next to you. Locals are incredibly helpful and resourceful. Don't be shy – ask for help if you need it. They might not speak your language, but a game of charades can work wonders in a pinch.

Pro Tip: Before you embark on any adventure, let someone know where you're going and when you plan to return. It's like leaving breadcrumbs for Hansel and Gretel, but with less chance of being eaten by a witch.

Now, don't let this list scare you. Patagonia is generally safe and welcoming. These numbers are just your safety net, like bringing an umbrella to keep the rain away. So go forth, explore, and create those once-in-a-lifetime memories. Just remember, in the land where the wind can blow you into next week, it's always good to have a lifeline or two!

Communication and Internet Access

Staying Connected in the Land of Disconnection

Welcome to Patagonia, where the Wi-Fi is as elusive as a puma and cell signals play hide-and-seek with your phone. But fear not, intrepid traveler! Here's your guide to staying connected (or blissfully disconnected) in this wild corner of the world.

The Cellular Tango:
In Argentina, the main players are Claro, Movistar, and Personal. In Chile, you've got Entel, Movistar, and WOM. But here's the kicker – coverage can be as patchy as a guanaco's coat. One minute you're posting glacier selfies, the next you're using your phone as a paperweight.

Pro tip: Get yourself a local SIM card. It's cheaper than international roaming and works better with the local towers. Just remember to bring an unlocked phone!

Wi-Fi Watering Holes:
Cities like Punta Arenas and El Calafate are pretty well-connected. You'll find Wi-Fi in most hotels, cafes, and even some public squares. But venture into the wilderness, and your Instagram stories might have to wait.

Fun fact: Some remote lodges have started offering "digital detox" packages. It's like rehab for your smartphone addiction, with epic views as a bonus!

The Cyber Café Renaissance:
Yes, they still exist! In smaller towns, cybercafés are having a moment. They're perfect for when you need to print that boarding pass or video call your mom to prove you haven't been eaten by a condor.

Satellite Saviors:
For the truly remote adventures, consider renting a satellite phone or GPS messenger. They're not cheap, but they're handy when you need to call for a helicopter because you've accidentally proposed to a sea lion.

The Patagonian Post:
Sending postcards? Adorable and retro! But be warned – the Patagonian postal service operates on its own special timeline. That "Wish you were here" might arrive after you're back home.

Language of Connectivity:
Learn these phrases:
- Hay Wi-Fi?" (Is there Wi-Fi?)
- Cuál es la clave?" (What's the password?)
- La señal está mala" (The signal is bad)

Use them often, with increasing desperation as you venture further into the wild.

The Upload Upload:
Found a rare spot with good Wi-Fi? Prepare for a traveler stampede that rivals the great guanaco migrations. Be a good digital citizen and limit your Netflix binges

Power Play:

Outlets in Argentina are mostly Type I, while Chile uses Type C and L. Bring a universal adapter, or risk having to rub two glaciers together to charge your phone.

The Disconnect Delight:

Embrace the digital detox! Some of Patagonia's best moments happen when you're not hunting for bars on your phone. Swap Google Maps for a good old paper map – they never run out of battery!

Radio Gaga:

In remote areas, radio is still king. Tune into local stations for weather reports, news, and the occasional llama traffic update.

The Telecom Trek:

Cell towers in Patagonia often have their own hiking trails. If you're desperate for a signal, follow the locals to the nearest high point. It's like a pilgrimage, but for Instagram addicts.

Café con Wi-Fi:

Some cafes offer better internet than others. Look for places with lots of laptops – digital nomads know where the good stuff is.

The Patagonian Preview:

Download offline maps, translate apps, and entertainment before you go. Your future self will thank you when you're trying to navigate Torres del Paine without cell service.

Emergency Ease:

Remember, even without service, your phone can still dial emergency numbers. It's like your digital guardian angel.

The Social Media Siesta:
Use your disconnected time to practice the art of conversation. Who knows? You might make a friend who doesn't need Wi-Fi to be interesting.

Cloud Conundrum:
The clouds in Patagonia are gorgeous, but they're not the kind that store your data. Backup your photos whenever you hit a town with good Wi-Fi.

So there you have it, your guide to navigating the digital landscape of Patagonia. Sometimes the best connection isn't to the internet, but to the breathtaking world around you. Embrace the spotty service as part of the adventure. After all, you came to Patagonia to disconnect from the world and reconnect with nature, right? Now go forth and explore – just maybe leave the live-tweeting for another trip!

Useful Apps, Websites, and Maps

Navigating Patagonia: Your Digital Toolkit

In the vast wilderness of Patagonia, where GPS signals sometimes wave the white flag, having the right digital tools can be as crucial as a good pair of hiking boots. Let's dive into the apps, websites, and maps that'll help you conquer this rugged paradise without ending up as guanaco feed.

First up, let's talk about the weather. In Patagonia, meteorologists probably have the most exciting job in the world. For up-to-the-minute forecasts that might actually be accurate, check out www.windguru.cz. It's a windsurfer's go-to, but in a place where the wind can blow you into next Tuesday, it's a traveler's best friend too. For a more comprehensive weather outlook, www.yr.no is your new weather guru. It's Norwegian, so you know it's serious about wild weather.

Now, onto navigation. While paper maps are great for that classic explorer feel (and don't run out of battery), digital maps can be lifesavers. Download Maps.me before you go. It's like Google Maps' rugged cousin, perfect for offline use when you're in the middle of nowhere – which in Patagonia, is pretty much everywhere. For hikers, Wikiloc (www.wikiloc.com) is a goldmine of user-uploaded trails. It's like a social network for people who prefer mountain views to Facebook views.

Speaking of hiking, if you're tackling the famous trails in Torres del Paine or Los Glaciares National Park, the Trekking Patagonia app is a must-have. It's like having a park ranger in your pocket, minus the awkward campfire songs. For those venturing into the backcountry, consider investing in what.3words. This app divides the world into 3x3 meter squares, each with a unique three-word address. It's perfect for precise locations when "by the big rock near the angry-looking guanaco" just won't cut it.

Language barriers can be as challenging as river crossings in Patagonia. While learning some Spanish is highly recommended (the locals will love you for it), having a good translation app is wise. Google Translate works well, but for a more Latin American flavor, try SpanishDict (www.spanishdict.com). It's not just a translator; it's a full-on language learning tool with slang and local expressions. You'll be chatting with gauchos in no time!

For those moments when you need to know what that weird bird is (no, it's not a small condor), iNaturalist is your go-to app. Snap a photo, and this citizen science platform will help you identify flora and fauna. It's like having a naturalist on call, without the khaki vest and binoculars.

Planning your Patagonian adventure? Rome2Rio (www.rome2rio.com) is brilliant for figuring out how to get from A to B, even if B is a remote estancia that's not on Google Maps. For booking buses and flights within Patagonia, check out Busbud (www.busbud.com) and Skyscanner (www.skyscanner.com) respectively. They'll save you from the hair-pulling frustration of navigating local transport websites.

For accommodations, besides the usual suspects like Booking.com and Airbnb, check out Hostelling International (www.hihostels.com). They have a network of hostels in Patagonia that won't break the bank and are great for meeting fellow adventurers. If you're feeling more adventurous, iOverlander is an app that shows camping spots, from established campgrounds to wild camping areas. It's like a secret map for those who prefer sleeping bags to silk sheets.

don't forget about safety. Absolutely essential, the Red Cross First Aid app is a must-have tool. It works offline and could be a lifesaver if you find yourself in a pickle. For those venturing into more remote areas, consider downloading what3words. This app divides the world into 3x3 meter squares, each with a unique three-word address. It's perfect for precise locations when "by the big rock near the angry-looking guanaco" just won't cut it.

While these digital tools are incredibly useful, they're not substitutes for common sense and proper preparation. Patagonia is wild and unpredictable – that's why we love it! Use these apps and websites to enhance your adventure, but don't forget to look up from your screen and soak in the jaw-dropping beauty around you. After all, no app can capture the feeling of standing before a towering glacier or watching the sun set over the Andes. Now go forth and explore, you tech-savvy adventurer!

CONCLUSION

Well, my fellow wanderer, we've come to the end of our Patagonian paper trail, but your real adventure is just beginning. We've trekked through towering mountains of information, navigated rushing rivers of recommendations, and camped under starry skies of local insights. But let me tell you, nothing – and I mean nothing – can truly prepare you for the raw, untamed beauty of Patagonia.

Remember when we talked about the wind that can blow you into next week? Well, get ready for it to blow your mind instead. Those glaciers we mentioned? They're not just big chunks of ice – they're nature's time machines, whispering secrets of ages past. And the landscapes we described? They're like paintings come to life, but even better because you get to walk right into them.

We've armed you with phrases to charm the locals, apps to keep you on track, and enough safety tips to make your mom proud. But here's the real secret: Patagonia isn't just a place you visit; it's a place that visits you. It sneaks into your soul when you're not looking, leaving footprints on your heart as surely as you'll leave footprints on its trails.

You'll find yourself doing things you never imagined. Maybe you'll share mates with a weather-worn gaucho, swapping stories as the sun sets over the pampas. Perhaps you'll stand in awe before Perito Moreno Glacier, feeling smaller than you've ever felt, yet somehow more alive than ever. You might even find yourself having a staring contest with a curious guanaco – trust me, they always win.

Sure, there'll be challenges. Your hair might look like it's been styled by the Patagonian wind (spoiler alert: it has). You might get lost and found and lost again, all in the same day. Your muscles will ache from hikes that seemed like a good idea at the time (and still were). But every blister, every wrong turn, every early morning wake-up call will be worth it.

Because here's the thing about Patagonia – it changes you. It reminds you how small we are in this big, beautiful world. It shows you that there's still wilderness out there, still places where nature calls the shots. It teaches you that sometimes, the best path is the one you make yourself.

So, my friend, as we close this guide, I'm not just inviting you to visit Patagonia. I'm inviting you to let Patagonia visit you. Pack your sense of wonder along with those hiking boots. Bring your curiosity as well as your camera. Open not just your eyes, but your heart to this land of extremes.

Are you ready? Ready to stand on the edge of the world and feel the wind in your hair? Ready to taste freedom in the crisp mountain air? Ready to write your own story in the vast book of Patagonia?

Well then, what are you waiting for? Patagonia is calling, and trust me, you want to answer. Lace up those boots, grab your backpack, and get ready for the adventure of a lifetime. The glaciers are waiting, the pumas are hiding, and somewhere out there, a perfect spot by a crystal-clear lake has your name on it.

Safe travels, amigo. May your journey be as epic as the land you're about to explore. And who knows? Maybe our paths will cross somewhere out there, under the big Patagonian sky. Until then, buen viaje!

Made in the USA
Monee, IL
26 March 2025